Morality and the Meaning of Life 7

MORALITY AND THE MEANING OF LIFE

In this series the following titles have been published:

1 Michael Moxter
Güterbegriff und Handlungstheorie:
eine Studie zur Ethik F. Schleiermachers
ISBN 90 390 0042 5

2 Bert Musschenga (ed.)
Does Religion Matter Morally?
A Critical Reappraisal of the Thesis of Morality's Independence from Religion
ISBN 90 390 0404 8

3 Philippe van Haute & Peg Birmingham (eds.)
Dissensus Communis
Between Ethics and Politics
ISBN 90 390 0403 x

4 Hub Zwart
Ethical Consensus and the Truth of Laughter
The Structure of Moral Transformations
ISBN 90 390 0412 9

5 Ina Praetorius
Essays in Feminist Ethics
ISBN 90 429 0590 5

6 Göran Möller
Ethics and the Life of Faith
ISBN 90 429 0699 5

THE END OF THE LAW

The Good Life:
a Teleological View

Stephen Theron

PEETERS
1999

D.1999/0602/14
ISBN 90-429-0725-8

Contents

Foreword

In the present work I have wished to isolate and treat more systematically what was already a major theme in my two previous books devoted particularly to ethics, viz. *Morals as Founded on Natural Law* and *The Recovery of Purpose*. This theme is that of the essentially teleological character of moral obligation as such, brought to light chiefly through attention to the fact that it is primarily the *ends* of action which oblige, and only secondarily the actions themselves or, still less, their formulation in terms of precepts. This doctrine is defended in many ways and places in Aquinas, as is his view that both happiness and God are more directly the *bonum honestum* than is human virtue, a view undercutting the attitude I have called moralism. Unfortunately these insights are not clearly reflected in the Thomist and clerical tradition. Thus in a sense this book is transitional as between my earlier emphasis upon an absolutist and restrictive interpretation of natural law theory, within which, however, I have increasingly distanced myself from a *rationalistic* ethical outlook, and a growing emphasis upon individual creativity and, above all, love and freedom as the true ethical goods. In line with this I would now suggest, in agreement with V. Bourke, that Aquinas was not in the first instance "a natural law ethicist", any more than was Aristotle. This view finds fuller expression in my forthcoming book, *Natural Law Reconsidered*. But the present work, as the sub-title indicates, serves to dispense with remaining vestiges of moralism in what, perhaps, should no longer be called a natural law ethics but an ethics of human nature as open to transcendent perfectibility, call this, with Berdyaev, the ethics of creativeness – or stress, with Fr. McCabe, its derivation from "the word as love".

I dedicate this book to the memory of Don Ramón García de Haro.

Introduction

Roncalli's Legacy

It is a minor tragedy of our times that the East European communists, no doubt unintentionally, succeeded in discrediting one of the most inspired of our modern documents, viz. the papal encyclical letter of 1963, *Pacem in Terris*. They did this by using its title, in the original Latin, as the name for a society of collaborationist or "fellow-traveller" priests operating in the then Warsaw Pact countries.

Now it would be a simple matter to demonstrate that such doctrinal and disciplinary indifference as this society stood for was at an opposite pole to the mind and intentions of the encyclical's author, Giovanni Roncalli, writing in his capacity as Pope John the Twenty-Third (1958-1963), the man who summoned the Second Vatican Council with its "opening to the world". Hence what the document signalled, rather, was that the time had come for the full manifestation of something latent in the Church from the beginning, as best expressed by the happenings recorded of the first (Christian) Pentecost in Jerusalem around the year 29. I refer to a capacity to address the whole human race, with its disparate languages, in a spirit of service and brotherhood. Hence this Pope's expressed hope and prayer for the new Council was that it would be as a new Pentecost or outpouring of the Spirit on all, bishops, observers, anyone interested, who took part in it. Opinions differ as to how far this prayer has been answered.

No doubt previous popes have exercised this capacity. What is clear is that the world became aware of this relationship in a new way during John's pontificate. This new awareness brings the papacy and the Church, and even the world, into what is effectively a new, a "post-modern" epoch, prophetically envisaged in Maritain's social and political philosophy, for example.[1] One needs therefore no apology for offering to a general readership a vision of renewal essentially Catholic (i.e. universal, according to the whole, *kat'holon*) without being sectarian. It is indeed part of the thesis put forward here, as will be presented in our first chapter, that society cannot long cohere without some binding doctrine or vision of positive character shared by the typical citizen.

The immediately apparent difficulty with this, however, is that in our time of mobility and uprootings there results in most places a *pluralism* in which

[1] Cf. Hans Kühner, *Neues Papstlexikon*, Fischer Bücherei, p.170. The same point is made in an essay of Hannah Arendt's.

the positive doctrines by which individuals supposedly live all resist one another. In desperation the idea is then put about (largely as a result of the military stalemate concluding the Thirty Years War at the Peace of Westphalia in 1648) that we can agree to disagree. Well we can, but that cannot be what holds society together, unless as containing a hidden positive aspect. In itself the stance is based either upon nihilism, a destructive lie, or upon a positive belief in human dignity with consequent respect for personal conscience. But this already amounts to a philosophy sufficiently positive to expose much of the cant of popular liberalism as empty self-contradiction.[2]

This philosophy, however, or so Roncalli and his three successors would have us believe, is part of the tradition of the Catholic Church. I make the qualification both as a concession to prejudice and as acknowledgement that, in the words of the Second Vatican Council itself, there have in the course of the Church's history at times appeared ways of acting inconsistent with these principles. Still, in so far as these principles appropriated by liberalism are legitimate they are taken from the body of a Christian tradition which brought them forth. As a matter of our history, as of our future, this is important, e.g. for an understanding of the American and French revolutions, of their *possibility*.[3]

There is of course a specifically liberalist perversion of these principles which is what we are combatting, such as the equation of freedom of conscience with a voluntarist irrationalism or the false idea that such indifference to truth, a pure negation, could be a foundation for human dignity. A society based upon these negations, we noted above, could not survive, since what they negate is the principle of society as such, viz. the *bonum commune* or common good. In this sense liberalism was the most radical enemy of society, issuing by natural process in the frankly nihilistic totalitarianisms of our post-liberal century. Now if this is clear, that our *de facto* pluralist society cannot survive on this self-defeating liberalist principle, that, in other words, the principle of a pluralist society cannot be pluralism itself, then something else has to supply the "unity of order" required for this diversity in unity. The candidature for this honour, however, as claimed by the various rationalist ideologies, whether based on Hegel, Darwin or Dewey, is surely discredited.

We must observe here, as essential to our inferences, that we do find, here in Europe and its offshoots, a society of definite character actually in existence. And it would follow from the argument so far that this cohesion which we call a society, Western society, can only have been founded in actual fact upon a principle such as that for which we are searching. In other

---

[2] Exposed as trenchantly in the Vatican Council II document *Gaudium et Spes* ("The Church in the Modern World") as anywhere else.

[3] Cf. J. Maritain, *Christianity and Democracy*, London 1945.

words, our principle must be there to be found in the traditions of actual society. But these are the traditions of the Catholic Church, itself the heir of Athens and Rome, but above all of Jerusalem.

So the main claim here is that the ministry and guidance of the Church is, in its nature, not restricted to believers in the full sense. It has shown this again and again in its history, and John XXIII and his successors have made this explicit. Again, it is clear off-hand that the papacy, rather than, say, the Dalai Lama, is the natural repository of spiritual wisdom among the European peoples.[4]

Now the Pope addressed his letter to "all men of good will". In papal eyes, however, for a person not a Catholic to be a man or woman of good will he or she necessarily must be suffering from an at least relatively non-culpable ignorance, either through not having heard or not having as yet understood the Catholic claim, or because assent is prevented through inherited prejudice or some other cause, such as a contrary conviction. Such ignorance (of the truth, as Catholics are obliged to see it: i.e. they must see it as a real ignorance) can be what is called "invincible", and need not be a bar to salvation, as Pius IX for one made clear in the last century. It is, in other words, the traditional Catholic position, developed within the ancient theology of the "baptism of desire".

Where people find this talk of ignorance disagreeable they would rather assume that the Church has itself gone over to some form of voluntarist liberalism. Yet the position is not very different from that which we all in general take to those who reject our own certainties, whatever they may be, though we may bend over backwards to avoid *calling* such people ignorant, so that witch doctors become "traditional healers", rather as prostitutes have become "sex workers", poor things. Catholics and their leaders are also affected by this verbal nervousness induced by the fact of pluralism, but where orthodoxy is preserved this is never more than a matter of style.

With its stress upon good will, therefore, the Catholic theory lays down the lines according to which cooperation is possible and to be hoped for. As a substantive body of social and ethical theory it is, as having taken into itself earlier sources, the prime source for those social and ethical principles which we so much need, though it can indeed be confirmed and added to by insights coming from other traditions too. In Europe itself the anti-tradition of nominalism and positivism is to be simply shunned as direct ancestor of statism, liberalism, Marxism and Nazism. The best Protestants have always followed the Catholic tradition of Augustine and Aquinas while, conversely, the issuing of late medieval voluntarism into sectarianism and these other movements shows that it does not belong with Catholic tradition.

---

4 See our *The Recovery of Purpose*, Frankfurt 1993, ch.9.

In restricting myself chiefly to the European and Western tradition I do not wish to obscure the fact that the opening of the modern popes has been to the whole world. But the treatment here is closely tied to meditation upon the development of *philosophy* as closely involved with specifically Western history[5] and indeed with Christian theology. It is as if in the rite and sacrament of baptism, with the demand that one be "born again", not just as a new start but in order to consciously affirm the implications of what has taken place also in the course of nature,[6] one consciously takes up the task of human advancement and salvation, which the Western institutions and ideologies, and they alone, however clumsily, never tire of fostering.

A further point is this. According to the Catholic system of our common ancestors Rome, ancient capital of the Western Empire, is set apart until the end of the world as the prime centre of unity in teaching and leadership. This refers to the teaching of truth, since it is as Bishop of Rome that the Pope succeeds to this charism as the successor of St. Peter, even if the actual city and its environs should one day be destroyed or rendered uninhabitable.

The relevance of this is that it is also the whole claim and *raison d'être* of Western *science* to be a teaching of truth, as discovered by sure empirical methods, man's truth, so to say. There is thus reason to argue that the West is bearer of the *very idea* of truth, that it stems, however distortedly, from the record of the man who "came to bear witness to the truth", as of a seed bearing many cross-related fruits.[7]

There is no way out of this, no way of making the presuppositions of the scientific mentality "cultural posits" in any normal sense, as if on a par with

---

[5] However, in *Africa, Philosophy and the Western Tradition* (Frankfurt 1995) I have given reasons for considering Western tradition as somehow normative, both because of the extent to which other portions of humanity are increasingly taking it over and on account of a universalizing impulse one can find within the culture itself, accounting at least in part for the rise of philosophy and natural science as disciplines of objectivity.

[6] Cf. Herbert McCabe, *Law, Love and Language* (in the US, *What is Ethics all About?*), London 1968, p.146f. on "the sacraments as an articulation of the deep meaning of human living. Baptism... is the sacrament of birth. Not just because it is analogous to birth but in the sense that it is the sacramental expression of joining the human race; it brings out what it actually means to be born. Baptism is not the sacrament of membership of the church, it *is* membership of the church; it is the sacrament of membership of mankind."

[7] Since this conviction of the reality of truth belongs to sound natural philosophy (a first principle of the speculative intellect, says Aquinas) it was of course not absent from the Greek tradition, either. We should note though that those who upheld it against the Sophists, such as Plato and Aristotle, mainly owe the survival of their writings, as against the sceptics of late antiquity, to their being championed by Church Fathers, including those heretical Fathers who took the manuscripts of Aristotle beyond the Empire, from where they were rescued centuries later by monotheistic Arabs. More typical of antiquity before Christ was Pilate's dismissive question, "What is truth?"

the Homeric gods as Quine would have it. Such philosophical evasiveness suggests a wish to avoid seeing the roots of Western science in the stability of Christian belief, nothing more. It is after this historical pedigree is made clear that people should discuss, if they wish, whether the Christian inheritance can be discarded without prejudicing the gains consequent upon its one-time acceptance, as one kicks away a Wittgensteinian ladder.

Chapter 1

Ethics, Values, Welfare

We can begin, indeed we can *only* begin, from where we are at. However the official representatives of the tradition which, in the Introduction, we expressed a wish to appropriate have often been strangely unwilling to begin from there, to make the effort, that is, to transport themselves in imagination into the situation of their potential disciples. Without that, however, no one is going to get to Tipperary, in any case a long way, as the song tells us, so that further obscuration should be kept to a minimum. But I would not myself be thought obscure for referring to that undoubtedly obscure Irish town. I have in mind, rather, the story of that picturesquely theoretical Irishman, no doubt himself a faithful traditionalist, who, when asked by a traveller the way to Tipperary, the very same, scratched his head before replying, with an air of delivering the fruit of a lifetime's meditation, "Well, if I were you I wouldn't start from here."

This man, even if we should find him attractive as a human type, is, we all know, wrong. We can only prescribe a remedy for our society's ills by starting from our society as it is. We cannot do it in the manner of some of the Romantics, for example, by holding up a picture, still less the too flattering picture usual in such a case, of the Middle Ages and proclaiming that that is how we should be. The Irishman was in effect telling the traveller that his projected journey to that town of song and fable was not possible. Or, if we give him for a moment the benefit of our doubt, we may think that his apparently nonsensical answer actually showed, rather, a more sure awareness of the extreme difficulty which that traveller was going to encounter, forced as he was to start from where he found himself, stuck in a bog perhaps.

And here we perhaps need this peasant wisdom, as we might call it. The reformer or revolutionary always starts from a difficult position, the position, namely, where he or those he addresses have to admit that a wrong course has been taken, have to form a resolve to go back, to repent. Repentance, indeed, is a revolutionary act, never a process of mere reform. This is because we cannot see in advance where it is going to lead us. This, indeed, is the typical mistake of those unrealistic officials to whom I referred. They go further than the Irishman. They want us, impossibly, to restore the past, to start from where we do not find ourselves, fighting wars with bows and arrows perhaps, or assured of the artistry and authority of nature, or able easily to enter into liturgical celebration as reflecting the rhythm of the seasons. Perhaps one is too hard on them. It is, however, a common temptation, and so one should always feel disquiet when one hears talk of a Restoration, whether of monarchy or church. Resisting this temptation, we have to start not only from the actual situation but from the actual vocabulary, the actual, current use of words, not of course in slavish acceptance but with an attitude at once informed and critical.[1]

Hence we will consider here some confusions regarding ethics and its place in social planning, rejecting the conception of ethics as a secondary constraint upon an existing welfare policy which is seen as ethically neutral. This, indeed, is just a consequence of the deep-seated paradigm of subjective value set over against objective fact. This paradigm is actually not much more than a slogan, to be understood, and so to say dissolved, in terms of the history of ethics and culture. There being a common end (the common good), if this is a fact, is a fact in apparent tension with the fact, as it has developed in history, of the existence of a pluralist society. But the tolerance and respect actually demanded by our common uncertainty, as a necessity of survival (which the experiment of totalitarianism tried to short-circuit), can only be grounded upon a discovery of human dignity.

In social philosophy today, however, certain assumptions have become widespread which frustrate attempts to introduce order into social planning and thinking, making them either harmful or futile. Nor has this happened overnight. So we need to identify both the assumptions and their provenance, if we are to understand where we may have gone wrong. Not all development is progress, as the term evolution might suggest. Revolution would then be forever unnecessary. But Christians, to take what is historically our most representative group, can never pretend that the events founding their religion were a natural evolution of Judaism, even if Judaism may have been destined from the first to issue in these events. The crucifixion of the Messiah, as in some sense willed by the latter, is the very essence of revolution, the "bringing to nought of the things which are, in order to exalt the things which are not." It is certainly not merely a matter of things happening with a greater speed.

We need, then, a full diagnosis before we can claim to be following a "scientific" social policy, rather than blindly imposing one new blueprint after another upon an ever more demoralised and resentful public.

*

* *

[1] There are indeed eternal truths, but the eternal truth (not the "old" truth) has to be ceaselessly integrated into new contexts. This is what "conservatism" denies, viz. newness of context. Thus, and for example, the "restored" Catholic hierarchy of 1850 in England and Wales was actually the setting up of entirely new sees, with Westminster, the modern capital, replacing Canterbury, one-time Anglo-Saxon capital of Kent.

One can indeed harbour a doubt about social planning in general, the very idea. One might fear that all such planners are really would-be "controllers"[2], out to totally dominate mankind in a *Brave New World* or *1984* scenario. The conceptual issues here would seem to belong to the philosophy of education. But what in any case causes trouble is that in practical deliberations a particular notion of *welfare* is all too often merely assumed. Welfare is not seen as needing itself to be grounded ethically and even metaphysically upon principles general enough to govern all *praxis*.

It can be misleading to call these principles *values*, as if they can be brought to bear upon a pre-existent but ethically neutral *praxis* forming part of a world of fact. There is no such "value- free" praxis, not even the praxis or practice of scientific research, since every agent acts for an end, and a researcher is, willy-nilly, an agent. This is why one cannot seriously oppose changing the world to understanding it, since *all* praxis involves a true or false understanding of what one is doing and why. This understanding, furthermore, *qua* practical, itself involves normal *theoretical* understanding of the *terms* used in one's practical reasoning. In other words there are not two rational faculties, the theoretical and the practical; it is rather that in practical reasoning reason as a whole *extends* itself to the job in hand. Hence there is no independently existing sphere or "universe" of values but what is good is always a being, some being or other. This is why Gabriel Marcel said that the very talk of values is often itself a sign of the devaluation of *being*:

> I would accordingly be inclined to make the following undoubtedly paradoxical affirmation that the introduction of the idea of value into philosophy, an idea virtually unknown to the great metaphysicians of the past, is as it were the sign of a fundamental devaluation of reality itself... It is true that we may think here of a certain compensation which, incidentally, remains imaginary, which seeks in an ideal manner, i.e. basically in the imagination, to find again that which on the level of reality one has a tendency to do away with....[3]

Thus welfare, as a practical concept, has to be integrated into a theory of man and the world. In fact we have the unhealthy situation that welfare policies are generally based upon an *unreflected* materialism merely patched up by ethical constraints at the points where it manifestly fails to hold together. Ethics is thus reduced to a kind of conscientious control (the nature and source of which defies explanation) upon the *means* used to achieve an end which is

---

[2] A term used by C.S. Lewis in *The Abolition of Man*, London 1943. Cf. R. Huntford, *The New Totalitarians*, London 1970.

[3] G. Marcel, *Les hommes contre l'humain*, p.127. Here Marcel seems to take issue with philosophers such as von Hildebrand and even, *prima facie* at least, Maritain (*Neuf lecons sur les notions premières de la philosophie morale*, Paris 1950), not to mention the Polish school from which Karol Wojtyla hies. He is, however, faithful to Aquinas. Cf. Leo Elders, *The Metaphysics of Being of St. Thomas Aquinas*, Leyden 1993, p.76.

already given, i.e. assumed, and which is hence an *imposition*, taken as unquestionable. No one has been consulted over the meaning or validity of the ends sought. This parallels the difference, in education, between indoctrination and the communication of an understanding.

In general the credentials of welfare, or of any social policy whatever, cannot be established if one insists on defining welfare or the social good in terms of a specified, quantitative material standard. Nor does one redeem the situation by speaking of a *right* to a certain living standard. For such language at once suggests unconditionality, this being the essence of a right or duty. Unconditionality, however, belongs to the natural end and purpose of life as fulfilling it, if it belongs anywhere at all, and so it has always to be enquired whether a given material standard in a given situation, e.g. one where there is starvation in some other country close by, will serve this end and purpose, usually interpreted, after all, as a common or shared good.

In effect, one can only speak rationally of such a right as part of a general network of rights, some of which are more fundamental than others. If this were not so then the required material standard could be achieved by sterilizing or simply liquidating the unfit or materially unprofitable. Such a material standard, after all, reflects a social or collective situation, to which, however rightful or desirable, one cannot sensibly sacrifice fundamental rights of the person, if these represent greater goods. So much for the family policy of the government of China. *Such* a notion of social planning simply confuses the elimination of starvation with the elimination of the starving. Unfortunately, however, this simple error is very prevalent in current thinking about the world and not only in China or India, where factors inhibiting the consequences of the error seem to have less force.

We need to enquire whether there is *any* notion of planned or rationalized welfare which is free of this crass error (of making the solving of social problems paramount over existing persons) and, if not, what might be the alternative. Are we not perhaps starting at the wrong end in planning a *society*? Is not society itself rather the end result of internalized ethical insight achieved by the persons making up society in their actual relationships to one another? They cannot be worked on from without in despite of their freedom. This "model", of welfare, communicates no energy, no personal commitment to keep it going. That, the commitment, is taken to remain the business of the planners alone, who hence become, after all, the controllers. This can occur even where a facade of democracy is maintained.[4]

---

[4] In 1973 the Swedish translation of Roland Huntford's hard-hitting exposure of social democracy in that country, subject to one-party rule for forty years, was mysteriously removed from *all* Stockholm's bookshops, little more than a day after it had appeared there. During the same period it was not possible to buy in Finland, also styled a democracy, translations of Solzhenitsyn's important attacks upon the neighbouring Soviet system.

The whole topic of human rights might thus seem to be philosophically vexed. Recently it has been claimed that such rights are merely fictions.[5] One need go less far and yet still claim that human rights are not specifiable in terms of material quantities. One cannot even specify them, it would seem, in terms of a simple inter-personal equality, since what is due to me cannot be assessed by comparison with what is due to, or *de facto* enjoyed by, my neighbour. For this would simply beg the whole question of anything being due to anyone. What, rather, is due to me consists in a certain *proportion* between that which is to be distributed and what I myself, or any other being, am. It is not the actual quantity distributed but this proportion which is *justum*, the just thing, and which is to be equal, i.e. the same (as a proportion), wherever applied. Thus someone who is half one's size or age might be owed half as much food, while more is due to a man from his own father than from a stranger. The alternative criterion of *needs* is quite useless since needs are evaluated in terms of those *ends* of life mentioned above.

What then remains of human rights? This, that they depend upon the dignity of human nature, as Kant tried so ineffectually to show with his voluntarist Kingdom of Ends. This, after all, was actually based upon a denial that there are any ends to human life (apart from human beings themselves!), a negative posture from which, as Sartre and others have since shown, no human dignity can be retrieved.

But human nature is expressed in persons, a person being one who takes charge, actually or potentially, of his own existence, in virtue of the intellectual and spiritual nature definitive of the human species. The dignity of a being endowed with cognition and volition derives from the sublime universality of the *ends* of these faculties, viz. the true and the good,[6] not from their having no end at all. There are thus first conceptions and inclinations natural to man, failing which we can have no science and no ethics.[7]

What man has a right to, in virtue of this sublime, always individualized nature, is individual respect; he or she is not negotiable, not eliminable. This conclusion, however, which we feel to be true, can only be established upon those ends of human nature mentioned, as these in turn rest upon man's ontological make-up, inclusive of his biology.[8]

The fact that there will always be philosophical debate about these matters does not make them optional, or inessential to the matter in hand. Everything is called in question at some time and there is no shortcut to establishing a philosophy of welfare. Essentially this is what the *ideologies*, as distinct from

[5] Cf. A.C. MacIntyre, *After Virtue*, London 1981; H. Veatch, *Human Rights: Fact or Fancy?* Baton Rouge & London 1985.

[6] Cf. Aquinas, *IV Sent., dist. 33, 1, 1.*

[7] Cf. Aquinas, *Summa theologica* Ia-IIae 10, 1; 94, 2.

[8] Cf. R. Spaemann, "Über den Begriff der Menschenwürde", *Scheidewege* 15, 1985/6.

philosophy, aspired, or conspired, to be, viz. shortcuts, final solutions to the perennial imperfections of human life. Hence they led only to more or less brutal violations of human dignity. So that way should now be considered closed, together with its disregard of or failure to grasp the nature of ethical thinking, established by Aristotle as a science.

*

* *

It was an impoverished *notion* of the ethical which made possible this development. First one separated the ethical "sphere" from any consideration of human ends and purposes (Hume, Kant). Then, in place of that, one set up the notion, unreflected within ethics, of utility. This was not seen as an end participated in by actions themselves, but as something apart from behaviour according to which the latter could be evaluated. Actually, though, human happiness, flourishing, itself consists in an activity, as *höchste Entfaltung der Sittlichkeit* (M. Grabmann). Talk of "basic needs" is a variant on this utilitarian view. In reality, though, the poor man who eats performs a moral act (*actus humanus*). There is always question as to why such and such a need is to be satisfied, why, ultimately, people are to be kept alive. Many utilitarian regimes have not known and do not know how to answer this question. All their talk of the quality of life serves primarily to deny quality, or worth, to living persons as such, i.e. unless they have *other* goods (besides mere life) to enjoy.

MacIntyre, in the work cited, shows well how this silence about ends in our reasoning followed upon the imposition of a mechanist world-view from the seventeenth century on. There are some interesting connections with Jansenist and Calvinist theology, its doctrine of total human depravity which excludes any type of Aristotelian concept of man as able to grasp the purpose of human life.

John Finnis, an Oxford legal philosopher, has attempted to break free from utilitarianism by reviving the doctrine of natural law.[9] In place of basic human needs he speaks of basic human goods. As goods they thus come under the purview of moral obligation. Finnis and his supporters, however, introduce a distinction between moral and non-moral goods, whereas for the older theory the good, any good, imposes at least a conditional imperative (*bonum est persequendum*: the or a good is to be pursued). This forms part of Finnis's refusal to recognize any objective hierarchy among human goods. They thus remain a somewhat arbitrary collection, a *list*, from which anyone can *choose*, setting up a "plan of life" in a pluralist society where we all play for different

---

[9] J.M. Finnis, *Natural Law and Natural Rights*, Oxford 1980.

goals according, inexplicably, to the same moral rules (inexplicably, if it be ends which specify actions morally). He pours scorn upon the classical arguments for there being one final purpose to all and any human life, viz. happiness. This was tentatively identified by Aristotle with study and contemplation, of which St. Augustine later said, "This only is desirable for itself." Aquinas transposes this to the vision of God, not to be achieved under temporal conditions but still the only thing that can satisfy a rational nature, even granted that the vision is in itself above the unaided capacities of that nature, since God, as the infinite being, can lie passive to nobody, but only be seen by loan of his own light freely given. Aquinas writes:

> True happiness does not consist in physical or social goods, or in moral virtues. The final good of man is to be found only in the contemplation of God and it is to this act that all human activities seem to be directed as to their last end... And so, if things are considered aright, it will be seen that all human states and occupations serve as means to the contemplation of truth.[10]

Christopher Dawson comments on this that "it might be said that culture is the necessary social discipline which subserves the higher ends of the spiritual life."[11] This end, anyhow, this contemplation of truth, seems very different from any basic human need as understood by welfare pundits. Yet unless there is some purpose to life of a nobility comparable to that of the contemplation of truth they cannot say why one should be kept alive at all. So the relief of the poor just cannot be effectively distinguished (by them) from the elimination of poverty. But this, we noted, can be achieved by eliminating the poor themselves, or even by preventing people from being born.

Embarrassed by this inability, and by the drastic courses of action to which it beckons them, such practitioners of welfare commonly introduce what we have called ethical *constraints*, even setting up some kind of ethical ombudsman or advisory council (one asks what could possibly qualify anyone for such a role). Here, probably by a majority vote, it will be agreed to abide by some principle or other which has by chance survived the general subversion of moral law in the modern period but which no one, on the premisses available, can rationally justify. Yet unless such justification can be found then these constraints, which have real if limited value, will not survive.

But who will inform the leaders of the state about the dignity and purpose of life as an end generating those ethical principles still slumbering in our consciences? Such informants could only be those who represent a tradition of wisdom and so have a consequent authority of some kind. It is actually of two kinds, intellectual and moral, in accordance with the dual character of *prudence* as a virtue of both intellect and will. There is no question then of

---

10 Aquinas, *Summa contra gentes*, III 37.

11 C. Dawson, *Religion and Culture*, London 1948.

filling a gap in the rational credentials of the tradition, since epistemic authority is in itself rational. It is of the nature, rather, of ethical knowledge as such to begin from first principles known to the wise (*sapientes*) as guardians of tradition imbued with *recta ratio*. Custom, *consuetudo*, both Aristotle and Aquinas declare, supplies the first principles of ethics, and to the extent that there is a stable human nature this must be so. By the same token it would be an error to think that good, as in "good is to be pursued", has no content.[12]

Regarding the natural relation of will to intellect we must observe that the popular, unreflected notion of freedom is deficient, even tainted today by the late medieval notion of *libertas indifferentiae*, a liberty of indifference between good and evil, this notion having being spawned by theological concern with a supposed divine test. In reality freedom is so far from being at the opposite pole to reason[13] that it is in fact its other face, since reason, like choice, holds itself *ad opposita*, between which opposites (or opposed things) it judges, in contrast to anything pre-determined. In this way freedom is the condition for specifically rational judgment. Hence the *irrational* choice is a first abrogation of freedom, as cutting off its root in reason, even though it be freedom itself which makes such a choice possible.

This rational character of freedom, and still more the free character of rationality, actually strengthens the ground for toleration, within limits, of what one sees as rational failure in the exercise of choice. Respect for conscience is recognition of the act(s) each person makes and has to make (that is the point) in forming his or her opinions, including judgments as to what is to be done. This applies even where the mental act concerned proceeds from a settled ignorance, since a person acting against conscience violates his nature, which as bearer of freedom as interpreted above (we can as well say bearer of rationality) has a worth higher than the whole of material nature. We may need at times to forcibly restrain the well-intentioned ignorant, but we may never attempt to force or cripple their minds. This is why torture in order to extract false or insincere statements is in itself a greater evil than cruel or wanton punishments or torments. But these principles, so stressed in our own times, should be viewed as secondary restraints upon the primary duty of overcoming ignorance, in oneself and others, and of repressing consequent bad behaviour, especially where the rights of others or the common good are manifestly affected, as in human sacrifice, abuse of children or the peddling of certain drugs.

Thus Thomas More, in *Utopia* (i.e. nowhere), while enjoining tolerance in his ideal imaginary state, yet found it necessary not to tolerate but to forbid the open spreading of atheism and disbelief in the soul's immortality (Kant's

[12] Cf. Aquinas, *QD de veritate* 11,1; *Summa theol. Ia-IIae* 51, 1&2, esp. *ad 2um*.
[13] As in R.M. Hare's conception in *Freedom and Reason*, Oxford 1965.

practical postulates). The mere holding of these opinions, however, was not to be punished. Such views, he thought, as taking away motive for observing the laws, endangered the common good, since the effort of obedience could no longer subserve the ultimate end of eternal life, of final satisfaction in the contemplation of truth mentioned above.

If moral life indeed has any dignity it gets it from being specified in this manner by this noble end, raising it above the incoherences of Kantian *Sittlichkeit*, and this is what founds the duty of tolerance. If we remove this ground for respect for consciences based on man's eternal destiny we make of him a "useless passion" (Sartre) and open the way, by undermining the objections, for totalitarian dictatorships.

Still, one may object, the contemplation of truth is not a likely ultimate purpose for what socialists are prone to call "the masses". The term, however, like the thought, shows contempt for human nature as does the associated materialism, and this contempt, bound to lead to such materialism, is illustrated in that Jansenist and Calvinist background traced by MacIntyre. But it is still true that "man does not live by bread alone", nor, conversely, in our search for bread do we become just animals, unconcerned with the moral good. In order to become not masses, but *a people*, men and women must, always and everywhere, have duties, ideals, aims. This was the meaning, as a genuine fruit of the Gospel, of the slogan of liberty, equality and fraternity. Such brotherhood (*fraternité*) presupposes ability to be a brother, but where there is not unitedness in the contemplation of truth there is not much brotherhood, but just an alternation of fawning and snarling in the dark.

*

* *

In resisting the doctrine of a sublime objective destiny for man, then, moralists have been prone to insist that ethics is concerned with what we ought to do, with our obligations (just a part of the *bonum honestum* of the older tradition). There has been much talk of the "moral sense", of the voice of conscience. But Freudian psychology and the Nietzschean philosophy upon which it was largely based are not alone in finding such notions easy to demolish. For a free spirit, anyhow, there is no sense in an obligation which is not either imposed for a purpose or itself participates in the fulfilment of that purpose (e.g. by the beauty or order created in discharging it). So no purpose, no obligations. One must at least say that in granting the validity of the "moral sense" one grants the reality of such an order and beauty, grants, at least, that there can be no meaningful virtue without hope.

What this simple truth excludes is the notion that ethics presents us with a set of principles which restrain, limit and tend to frustrate our purpose, but which we must, as we say, respect. If ethics contradict our purpose, indeed, then there is something wrong with our purpose. On the other hand, there cannot in reason exist an ethics to which a set of purposes is not intrinsic, and which perhaps need to be clarified first of all when formalizing the system. In fact, however, this will involve clarifying that a purpose, as mentioned above, rests upon man as man, i.e. it is natural to him. It is a matter of recognizing the purpose which man naturally has, his natural needs, not of voluntaristically selecting it or them. Hence any purpose is ultimately to be judged by its congruence with human nature. Does it fulfil our aspirations? Is it, for example, natural to some people to be homosexual or are they sick, crippled? In the latter case we may reason to legal toleration of some of their activities but we will not approve their way of life and those in the field will have a duty to search for cures, means of prevention and so on.[14] One might here also consider the question of voluntary lunacy. Can one, and if so may one, choose to be mad, opt for an obsessive life-style, an enthusiasm? It would be hard to reply in the negative.

The purpose of all ethics, all morals, is the achievement of human flourishing (eudaimonia), not by being technically instrumental to such flourishing but as specifying our actions as morally good. If, for example, ethics should forbid birth-control or abortion programmes then this *means* that such programmes are hostile to human flourishing, to the achievement, in particular, of the *common good*, something quite different from the aggregate good. The same applies to simple injustice, i.e. that it is ultimately explicable, as wrong or evil, in this way. It is in this way, indeed, that evil, moral evil, is seen to be a more basic and general category than injustice. Viewed as law the whole corpus of morality falls under legal justice (i.e. *justitia legalis*), but law, even such law, is subsequent to the identification of the good, this being just what we have been saying, viz. law and ethical principle depend upon the identification of purpose or end, without which no law is given. Now we can see why good, for its part, has the meaning (*ratio*) of end, that which is sought. So it is that the judge who permits the lynching of a man known to be innocent, like Billy Budd, that "the whole people perish not" or because one is at war, harms the common good. If he did not, then there would be nothing wrong with such a lynching, it would not be unjust. Justice would indeed be the advantage of the stronger, as Thrasymachus asserted long ago.

Let us suppose that we be convinced by these considerations as to the nature of ethics; what difference might it then make to our view of the role of ethics in the public service? The model of the *pluralistic* society might seem

[14] There is also the further question, is it natural to the species, is it consonant with the *common* good, that there exist such a minority, even if homosexuality were found natural to them (by genetic formation) as individuals, i.e. should it be tolerated by the community or should active homosexuals be placed on a par with pedophiles, whose spontaneous wishes carry no weight with us.

instantly endangered. An objective hierarchy of ends commits us all to a common pursuit, the common good in other words. But if it has been shown that morality essentially imposes such ends, in logical priority to the imposition, or prohibition, of those actions which are means to, or necessarily avert from, those ends, then we have not much choice, apart from ditching morality altogether, if this be possible. Perhaps it has been ditched long ago. Those who believe this see liberalism as a decomposition or atomization of the social body. It is, anyhow, of the essence of a society that it have a common goal, while an indifferent freedom to pursue different goals cannot itself be such a goal.

The political conclusion is inevitable. There can be no pure welfare state in the sense of a state limited to an economic commitment to material satisfaction of presumed needs, with no relation to the worth and dignity, or lack of it, of human life. The common aims of society have to be declared in accordance with this dignity, and the external instance which regulates and interprets these aims and their adoption cannot have other than a central position and standing, since the principles which it safeguards must be directive of the executive itself. For the executive, to be truly political, directive of the whole people to its common end, must be guided by an acknowledge wisdom, a hierarchy of values which will surely have its professional guardians, just as we have these for our mental balance, bodily health and education. Otherwise we are demanding that the ministers of state themselves, the kings, be philosophers (the opposite of the Platonic extreme), a situation reflected in the noticeable servility before the law of post-Lutheran societies.

A purely negative freedom not to be bound by any natural end, so that we set up our own ends in "plans of life", would not, we saw, be a possible object for such a directive wisdom. A freedom to go nowhere is no freedom, and the attempt, surely futile, to rob the human race of its ennobling end and purpose does no one a service. The stalemate of disagreement over essentials which gave rise to our modern pluralism was in itself a negative phenomenon which could only tend to slow down or halt any progress of an ordered kind. It cannot be an end or ideal. We still have to strive to achieve life's purpose and this must at times include facing up to conflicts over our beliefs, at home and internationally. Something has to be found for any society still in existence to unite it once again, as we know it did not come *into* existence without an original purpose. This something cannot however be just anything, such as fomenting a hatred of foreigners. A wrong or inadequate aim will in time only fracture society all the more. Truth, whatever it is, must be pursued and held.

*

* *

So, in our actual situation, there has to be a dialogue, but dialogue has presuppositions. There is a perverted conception of freedom of opinion which subverts any possibility of dialogue, since it subverts the concept of opinion as such. This perversion consists in the reduction of the notion of an opinion to that of an *attitude*, which can be changed at will. We seem to incline to this frame of mind when we preface our statements with "the way I see it", as if seeing were a function of one's subjectivity (it is, rather, a "success" verb), or "I feel that..." instead of "I think". At such a level, however, an opinion has not been achieved and so it is clear that no argumentative dialogue, in the sense of rational dispute transcending the rhetorical, can take place, since no opinion has been asserted. There is no reason at all, of course, to expect that if such a gang of sceptics sit down and talk they are any the more likely to reach a positive consensus with any claim to truth, this being foreign to their habits of thought. Rather, the danger is thereby increased of an arbitrary procedure being imposed upon the rest of us by sheer force of will reflected in a majority of votes, as if there were nothing else in the universe to limit the scope of such voting, such as the rights of the innocent, for example.

One can of course consider something *hypothetically*, as in a scholastic disputation, but this is by definition theoretical. The practical reason would not be involved, as it must be in a dialogue envisaged as a means to solving society's practical problems, these being the same as its *ethical* problems in the sense of "ethical" outlined above.

For there to be an opinion there has to be a possibility of a judgment concerning the true and the false, and for there to be this possibility there have to be some first, naturally known (*nota per se*) principles from which the reason starts out, these being necessary for any conceivable science (debates about "foundationalism" should not obscure this point). What has bid fair to destroy ethics as the science of the practicable has been the loss of a reflective grasp on these first principles, even though they cannot but continue to operate in our daily transactions. These principles are grasped in an instinctive reflection upon our natural inclinations, expressed corporately in the customs of human society viewed as a whole. There is no other possible source for them, no *a priori*, no "moral sense" or conscience operating in a void, although we can of course seek to ground the truth of these first principles metaphysically, as with all the sciences.

It is therefore of the first importance for the scientific and rational character of the ethical, which is surely admitted where one admits concern over the ethical quality of welfare services, that an ordered hierarchy of these inclinations of human nature be visible, since it is upon this that the ordering of ethical laws and the consequent tabling of virtues and vices are founded. One cannot do better than quote a summary of these inclinations and their order as given by Thomas Aquinas:

> First, there is in man an inclination based on the aspect of his nature which he has in common with all substances — that is, that everything tends according to its own nature to preserve its own being. In accordance with this inclination, those things by which human life is preserved and by which threats to life are met fall under natural law. Second, there is in man an inclination to certain more restricted goods based on the aspect of his nature which he has in common with other animals. In accordance with this inclination, those things are said to be of natural law "which nature teaches all animals", among which are the union of male and female, the raising of children and the like. Third, there is in man an inclination to the good based on the rational aspect of his nature, which is peculiar to himself. For example, man has a natural inclination to this, that he might know the truth concerning God, and to this, that he might live in society. In accordance with this inclination, those things relating to an inclination of this sort fall under natural law. For instance, that man should avoid ignorance, that he should not offend those among whom he must live, and other points relevant to this inclination.

Now, as has been recently emphasised by MacIntyre, Finnis and others, as being "quite certain", this was "the general form of the moral scheme", prior to a collapse into incomprehension due principally to the over-running of the field by anti-philosophical, late-medieval and Reformation *theologies*. As analysed by Aristotle the theme was threefold in its presuppositions. There was

> some account of potentiality and act, some account of the essence of man as a rational animal and above all some account of the human *telos*.[15]

MacIntyre further points out that the scheme "is added to but not essentially altered" when placed within the framework of one or other of the main theistic beliefs. What *did* alter it, however, was such things as the paradoxical, nominalist theses about the total depravity of human nature and hence of reason, tied to a doctrine of the *potentia absoluta Dei* which might seem to imply the total depravity of God as having the power to declare good evil, evil good. *Such* a God, metaphysically considered, could not, and so does not, exist. Still less could he reveal himself credibly, since he is understood as being free to lie.

Now despite these transgressions of some theologians at that time it is yet true that the main champions today of this broad ethical scheme, inclusive of a corresponding notion of the human essence and *telos*, are the representatives of the main religious traditions, Christianity in particular supplying the basic premise for any enduring humanism. The 1789 prescription of brotherhood, we have noted, went beyond classical ideals of civic friendship, inviting society to joy, i.e. to achieved human flourishing, as perceived (beforehand) by Schiller, in a quasi-musicalization of politics from which we would regress to

---

[15] MacIntyre, *op. cit.* p.50.

our common loss. Our situation now calls for a "civilization of love", as attested to in all our modes of communication.

From this point of view the recent (1993) recognition of Christian values by the government of Sweden as somehow fundamental to their society's character was most welcome. In so far as the Christians, in a given society, might be identified as the main bearers of ethical tradition as philosophically evaluated there is then scope for some kind of shared ecumenical drive from the side of believers to set society on course towards humanization, human flourishing.[16] A reconciliation of the laity and clergy might be called for, implying also a revision of that view of the relation of philosophy to theology suggesting, even within the Christian community, that there are two competing sources of wisdom. How they are ordered to one another must be enquired into again.

In so far as unity might not be preserved within this ecumenical drive, thinking again of those rogue theologians of earlier times, intra-Christian dialogue, in which, however, all of a society characterized by Christian values might participate, must take place. But where so much is at stake, conflict cannot be excluded. Indeed one has to say that the Peace of Westphalia of 1648, with its militarily enforced negative mutual tolerance, brought a respite but no final solution or even progress in solving society's problems. The nominalist denial of natural law which was current in much late-medieval and Renaissance theology and which has passed into modern liberalism remains an obstacle, we have argued, to an understanding and consequent prosecution of human flourishing such as could lead to a humanized, non-arbitrary and hence ethical approach to welfare. Liberalism opens the way to tyranny, open (1933) or hidden.[17] Based exclusively upon securing prosperity for a given nation (and thus reinforcing that hostility to genuine opinion which engenders liberalism in the first place, opinion being an irrelevant spiritual interference with this materialism), liberalism is unable to supply the citizens with any motive for sharing their surplus as, in the nature of things (poverty in surrounding nations, consequent immigration etc. etc.), it is forced to lurch from one hypocritical, face-saving gesture to another, thereby exasperating the selfishness and passive dependency which it has so assiduously nurtured in those very citizens, along with the false consciousness of any number of spurious "rights".

---

[16] This is really the ideal of the various Christian Democrat parties, however it may at times be distorted in practice.

[17] Cf. A. de Tocqueville, *Democracy in America* (1830), New York (Mentor) 1956, on the "depraved taste for equality" which "reduces men to prefer equality in slavery to inequality with freedom." He also argues that the tyranny of majorities is *ipso facto* the most powerful and oppressive of tyrannies. Cf. our *Africa, Democracy and the Western Tradition*, Frankfurt 1995, ch. XI, "Human Rights".

This returns us to the proposal of a civilization of love, where the citizens find energy to provide for the welfare of one another, beginning with their own families, but also energy to devise better subsidiary systems of mutual care. Regarding this energy, many philosophers have wished to place at the centre of their ethics that Golden Rule of the Gospels which they erroneously present as a command *not* to do to others what one does not wish them to do to oneself, i.e. as a mere heuristic device for finding out a right but inert rule of action.

This may be good as far as it goes. But the commandment taught in the Gospels, "on which hangs all the law and the prophets", has little or nothing to do with any such rule-following, enjoining rather an active programme of love, viz.

> *Do* to others what you would wish them to do to you,

in conscious imitation of the heavenly Father who "sends his rain on the just and the unjust", seeking a new life in giving without measure. Now one cannot live like this as following a written text. It is rather a response to the Father's revelation of himself in Christ, upon which is founded all that is positive in European civilization (in origin not an ethnic but a sacro-political entity).

This is a much more energetic programme, corresponding to our idea of love as expanding action rather than to a limitation placed upon our activity by rational law. Can it be denied that this more active approach, by the way, was part of the original inspiration of welfare?

Even if this energy can seem to endanger pluralism there can yet be no freedom without it, or something of it. Love indeed is the only way to go, as being the cement of the social edifice, and it is ruinous to substitute some tribal solidarity of blood or language for it. Indeed, one then flees from politics itself.

So for our societies, in our historical situation, it would be folly to continue to neglect or seal off our specifically theological traditions. We have to call upon the representatives of these traditions, therefore, as entrusted with the divine law, to teach us, and not merely to exhort. Thus reinstating "the spiritual power", in a way consistent with religious liberty, will provide salutary moderation, at the least, of the horrendous powers of modern governments, besides healing one of our most fundamental schisms, that between priest and people.[18] This is surely a prerequisite to those international and interconfessional reconciliations which must surely form part of our programme of solving the ethical problems of the welfare state, at least in countries which hope to have influence in the wider world of the European Community and beyond.

Such a wish indeed witnesses to a *will* to solve the paralysing problems experienced in individual countries, even at the cost of renouncing ancestral

[18] Cf. our *The Recovery of Purpose*, Frankfurt 1993, chapter IX.

prejudice where necessary. Duty above all, indeed, as is imprinted upon the Swedish coinage (*Plikten framför allt*), but we should understand, again, that our duty is based upon the inclinations and consequent goals of human nature, in virtue of its inherent and hence obligating dignity. This position, hard to refuse, is yet only vindicated in a religious or at least theistic philosophy as the one valid charter for humanism, having corresponding practical consequences for society.

Chapter 2

The Origin of Morality

Having begun from where we are at, as we expressed it, we now need, all the same, to step back a little. Our theme is that of ethical orientation, of ordering the priorities. It is then a question of behaviour, and even of a code of behaviour, since all reasoning, and hence all writing, is concerned with the universal, the idea. That is to say, it is bound to issue in a kind of code or cipher, a net to catch all kinds of fish within a certain range. This is why reason, to be true to its task of one-to-one representation, is also committed to the task of decodification of its own structures, not so much in what would seem the contradictory project of a critique of reason but in the much more difficult task of elaborating a theory of analogy, of the difference between things as known in notions and things as they are in themselves. This is what Aristotle discusses in the most difficult parts of his *Metaphysics*, the claim being that things in themselves are given to us through our senses (*judicium sensus est de re*), this being as much a verdict upon the *concept* of thing-in-itself as it might be an over-confident claim to physiological knowledge (of the senses). As such it is capable of meeting Kant on his own ground.

The code of behaviour as traditionally set by human societies after, no doubt, repeated acts of reasoning upon similar situations but not always, perhaps, complemented by the corrective to be supplied by awareness of the *analogies* of things and situations, and of the corresponding need for virtues of discrimination reaching beyond the letter of the law, this code is what is called morality. What we have said already partly explains how it is that people can experience morality as something superimposed *after* life has been given, so to say, this being a precondition for the further judgment that morality *cripples* life. The Nietzschean and post-Nietzschean critique is well known. However, it would seem to follow from what has been so far advanced in these pages that this critique is, at least in great part, a consequence of that impoverished notion of morality which followed upon the separation of ethics from metaphysics and anthropology generally brought about, on one account, by a wish to safeguard the arbitrary freedom of God to command as he might wish. This, however, was a matter of the theologians keeping the debate at the level of Plato's *Euthyphro* and coming up with the opposite answer to his, even though the materials for solving the problem lay to hand in the Augustinian (and even Platonic) doctrine of the eternal law (*lex aeterna*). God is perfectly free and the law reflects his being, *is* indeed his being as governing the world; so as good is being, i.e. good is whatever God is, so law is the code of reality, without which the human goal will not be reached. It does not cripple life, it points the way to it. "This do and thou shalt live", i.e. as a natural consequence and not simply because one thereby avoids offending an irascible God, a God almost totally de-natured in the voluntarist theologies, in despite of all his efforts to reveal that nature to us (e.g. "God is love" and so on).

We intend, all the same, to give due weight to the existence of this critique of morality, which imposes the task of as it were restoring the *credentials* of morality. Accordingly we will begin by asking, in our own way, the kind of wondering question most often put by psychologists, social theorists or utilitarian philosophers who see morality as a restrictive structure born out of ignorance or the necessities of survival, necessities, they feel, imposing a need for concealment of the truths of freedom by means of false reports of prohibitions and so on, i.e. by a dampening, for social reasons, of our most vital impulses. This is the whole tension and contradiction of Freudian theory, followed also by those philosophers who on utilitarian principles advocate the continued fostering in society of moral beliefs which they personally consider false. The ideologists were the natural successors to these engineers of behaviour.

The question such people ask, in consciousness of being able to supply the answer, is this: what is the origin of morality? How was this secondary impulse, rather like Freud's death instinct, able to arise and oppose itself to the primary impulse of life? Such a question does not come naturally to those in the older, teleological tradition. Still, we shall, in deference to the prevailing atmosphere, ask and attempt to give our own answer to this question.

*

* *

It is not, then, difficult to see that anything in this world, and even the world itself, has an origin. The same axiom, after all, is employed even by those who persist in imagining a world of ideas somehow more immediate to us than the world in which we in truth and in fact find ourselves. For then there is always question of the origin of our ideas and even, last absurdity, of the origin of our idea of origin.

Yet we should note that the actual posing of the question as to the origin of any given reality itself amounts to the exclusion or postponement of all other possible questions about origins, e.g. about the origin of something else. This postponement, therefore, itself indicates something which that same enquiry must take into account. We have to know, or at least be enquiring after, why we are asking about this particular thing.[1]

The spontaneous answer that one just wants to know is not merely legitimate. It is even mandatory. Not only, as Aristotle saw, do all men desire to know. They even *should* so desire, at least to know those things *worth* knowing, singled out by *studiositas*, a virtue, as against mere curiosity. What this mandatoriness indicates, I wish to note at this point, is that a theoretical question as to the origin of morality, for example, carries with it no entitlement or power to suspend the ordinary moral imperatives employed in any practical reasoning, the exercise, that is to say, of those virtues for the most part falling under that studiositas already mentioned, such perhaps as ardent love of truth, prudence and fairness in investigation, thoroughness in completing the enquiry and so on. Practical reason controls the exercise (praxis) of theoretical reason, well or badly, never neutrally. We need morality, it seems, for the projected investigation of morality.[2]

This answer, however, that one just wants to know, gives the reason for, explains and causally grounds (my equivalences are deliberate) any activity of questioning at all. It is thus part of the answer, as genus to species we might say. Like genus though, questioning which is not specified is a mere *ens rationis*. It is the specific question, his own question, about which the questioner needs to be clear. Why is he asking it? What does he seek? More generally, what are the principles of selection of those questions which actually come to be asked?

In posing any question one introduces a dualism between the questioned aspect of the world and all its other features. This dualism, by the principle of sufficient reason, must have some ground in one's mind. Even if we raise the question about the origin of the world as a whole then we place the world as a whole at a distance from everything and every grouping of things within it, this being precisely the metaphysical stance.

It is indeed so that there being a world is quite distinct from whatever is in it, as, among the philosophers, is existence from essence. But if this most basic of questions yields such an awful dualism, which we name the world's contingency, then there need be little doubt of there being some comparable division behind any other question about origins.

So much is this consideration taken as truth, indeed, that we situate or interpret the questions we hear in accordance with it. For example, if asked what is the origin of teeth one does not, where one has confidence in one's questioner,

[1] The reason we ask why we ask the questions we do and not other ones is that our answer, to be true, must be the whole truth. The regress extends no further.

[2] Cf. St. Anselm, *De veritate*: He who thinks truly (*quod est*) thinks as he ought to think, and thus his reasoning is right (*recta*).

merely tell him not to be silly, we all have teeth. One supposes rather, however "out of the blue" the question may have come, that he is putting a question of a biological or evolutionary, perhaps biochemical sort. One supposes this because it is only against such a background that someone sane might be mentally distinguishing the genesis of teeth from all the other becomings in the world.

Having confidence, indeed, is simply acknowledging the shared rational world in which alone questioning is possible. Thus, to take a second example, if someone asks what the origin of work is then one supposes him to be meditating a world in which such a necessity would have no place and not finding it inconsistent. In answer, therefore, one will probably find oneself talking about something like the fall of Adam. The brutal "How could it be otherwise?", that recusant habit of disallowing questions, this, when it is not pathologically self-protecting, must always include a failure (perhaps innocent) to understand the question, genuinely stupid questions being perhaps not so common as assumed. The person's asking the question, whatever it is, reflects the opening up of some division in his mind, often called wonder. He or she asks, perhaps, why there are both men and women, and here indeed the brash rejoinder (how could it be otherwise?) in one sense could be a request to describe his wonder in more detail as a prelude to getting better to grips with his question, even though it might appear to be challenging him to drop it. But if he is not easily intimidated he may anyhow reply "I will tell you how" and launch into Plato's description of the androgyns or Milton's picture of Adam before the creation of Eve, two ways in which things could be otherwise.

In a contingent world one can wonder about anything, the principle of non-contradiction, the four seasons, the extension of matter. However it is well known that questions, besides signalling wonder, also raise doubts. Yet it is debatable whether every question both signals wonder and raises a doubt, or whether, on the contrary, any given question can only do one of these things. The hostess who asks, "Would you like some more wine?", where this is a serious question, contrives to raise a doubt where, one may well feel, no doubt was legitimate. One may be as annoyed at having to demonstrate that one still wants more in the face of this gratuitous suggestion of abstinence as a man may be at having to explain that he does not beat his wife when asked if he has stopped doing it. A similar objection might be made to the staging of a debate about abortion or about the rights of a given group, Jews say, the objection being that what is controversial in fact, if it is, is not thereby controversial as of right. The man who insists that in philosophy one questions everything, unless he carefully qualifies his statement, may be suspected of not having seen this second effect of the posing of a question, viz. that it is the concealed assertion of an uncertainty. Hence one can question whether one should question everything.

But, it may be objected, one is talking of yes-no questions rather than of what-questions, like what is the origin of morality. This is not entirely so, however. Many what-questions in appearance are yes-no questions in substance (i.e. in the intention of the speaker), e.g. By what right are you driving this car? (i.e. Have you a licence?); What are your views on nuclear power? (i.e. Are you for it?). "What is your name?", by contrast, raises no yes-no doubt as to your having a name, though it can sometimes signal a suspicion of memory-loss. It can all the same indicate that the questioner does not know your name and this can at times seem as gratuitous as requiring assurance that one wants more wine.

So questions revolve around wonder and doubt. Yet while wonder, one would think, can be allowed at anything, doubting questions, especially if idly put, e.g. in interrogative echo of information just supplied, are often distinctly irritating. In academic philosophy, too, there is often temptation to an idle raising of doubt, since people need controversies to keep them going. The claim of Descartes, of course, was that his "methodic doubt" was not idle.

In regard, then, to the question of this chapter we might wonder whether wonder or doubt were paramount. Morality is as isolable a phenomenon as any other for the purposes of wonder. In fact a certain parallel suggests itself here between the contrast of wonder against doubt and the Aristotelian contrasting of distinction against separation. For in wondering about morality one does not commit oneself to any weakening of a putatively indissoluble bond in reality between the human essence or life and human morality. One might well conclude precisely to that. Yet the question does seem to invite a doubt, or possibly the quashing of a doubt which the questioner was unwillingly entertaining. The doubt, or fear, seems to be, again, that at some point morality was perhaps super-imposed upon a previously complete, self-sufficient but non-moral humanity. If so then it might even now belong to the non-essential super-structure of life, a possibly harmful effect of civilization, like the flour used in white bread. Thus the word "origin" easily suggests a temporal commencement. In so far then as the question immediately reflects a particular view of life which might be ill-conceived, e.g. if it echoed a contractualist or initial "state of nature" view of man and morality, then the question may itself be ill-conceived. In the face of that possibility, however, we might apply the principle which we described earlier and interpret the question positively as asking for an account of the *role* of morality in human life, or of the nature of moral tradition.

The question as to the origin of morality, then, might appear similar to a question as to the origin of the Reformation, or of anything else we might well have done without. One says "we" but there is, of course, in any case, a question as to the origin of man himself, which some may think the universe might well have done without. It is nonetheless surely understood that when we are asking the question about morality, as about the Reformation, we are asking about its origin in *human life*. This means, again, that we are in some sense asked to conceive of human life without it. But in what sense? In a sense like that in which we might be asked to conceive of human life without the Reformation, as at least one novelist, to say nothing of Nietzsche's meditation on the topic, has attempted? Surely not. We would have more difficulty imagining a race without morality than we would in dreaming of a tribe of rational beings with only one foot, for example. For we might just as well speak of a tribe of rational beings without rationality.

It is true that in the wake of the evolutionary theory we do find ourselves talking at times as if we had no difficulty separating men from their rationality. Man began to use tools, we say, or his brain, in such and such an era, started to develop the ability for conceptual thought. Now I should say that it is an absurd fantasy that *brains* ever could have ability for conceptual thought, but what is noteworthy is that no concrete man, such as John Smith, or Neanderthal Nickie, is so spoken of. If we were to ask who this man was who, full grown or approaching his dotage, could not yet think or talk, the most likely answer would be that he wasn't anybody. Rationality is inseparable from the human essence, even if vivid imagination leads us at times to speak as if this were not so, just as the unlettered, says Aquinas, speak of the angels as if they had bodies.

Therefore, and despite forms of speech suggesting the contrary, it might well be the case that morality too is inseparable from the human essence, precisely because morality is inseparable from rationality. This, saying this, raises the question of freedom of choice, of free will, since morality is inseparable from rationality just inasmuch as freedom is inseparable from rationality. Moral judgment is only applicable to free agents, potential subjects of praise or blame; it is in *this* sense that we talk of acting well or badly meaning by this a good or bad use of our liberty. What *moral* judgments are are judgments as to this.

Here though we encounter widespread notions of a rationality with which freedom has nothing to do. Thus all kinds of rational behaviour are ascribed to mechanical computers, not, however, without compensating fantasies about computers *wilfully* "taking over", though there is no possibility, on any sound theory of will, that computers have wills.[3] A rational being is a free being is a responsible being is a (the) proper subject for moral judgment. The whole idea of a *balanced* rational judgment is one in which the balance is not tilted by outside (in the sense in which passion, too, is outside reason), determining fac-

[3] Thus D. Dennett's bracketing of computers with animals and humans as "intentional systems" (*Brainstorms*, Montgomery 1978, p.11)is best seen as a *reductio ad absurdum* of the postulate of "artifical intelligence", obedient to the model of monist naturalism.

tors. That is, it is a free, uninfluenced judgment.[4] This, in fact, is already included in the very idea of judging.

Yet morality has to do with action. It is acts that are moral, as they are human (*actus humani*), and the virtues are precisely habitual abilities (*habitus*) to perform good actions. Morality, that is, is practical. Reason, though, is theoretical, only becoming practical, we noted, by extension. This extension, however, is not human by some afterthought. For man always had to act, as he had always in his thinking to recognize the universal in the particular. Morality is thus the point at which reason impinges on the world, so that it can even refer to the *exercise* of thinking (theoria) itself, the "highest form of praxis", said Aristotle, in so far as it is an activity of human beings in the world.

Still, just as we noted that a question in abstraction from a question about this or that was a mere *ens rationis*, so it is with morality, if abstracted from this man's or this nation's morality. That there should be morality wherever there is man should be quite clear once we know what we are talking about, yet talk of an origin, nonetheless, suggests concrete reality, the origin of that particular morality particularly we happen to have.

But do we have such a particular morality and what anyhow is meant by having a morality? One must take the second question first. If I have a morality then that surely means that I am expected, or at least expect myself, even intend, to act in a certain way, a way we might speak of as *corresponding* to the morality (to its "norms", perhaps). Correspondence suggests the idea, after all, of some kind of a map, no doubt a conceptual map which we can consult in what we would have to say is our memory. But there is not much point in saying that unless we have some kind of theory as to how it got into our memory. Not only that, but we need a theory as to how it got into our memory carrying with it the highly *authoritative* credentials without which any talk of morality would be idle. There are many things in our memory with which we feel no need at all to correspond, and even things which we know we should avoid or contradict.

Morality, then, is taken as some kind of mental possession, a *knowledge* of what kinds of action are to be done, what avoided. We should realise though that when we say that we undercut that whole crop of philosophical theories, of "autonomous" ethics, which would begin where such a morality (*mores*, customs) leaves off. For what these theories amount to are *sets of directions*, somewhat high-minded, for each person to forge morality anew, though this need not exclude, and is often hoped to include, coincidence of these autonomous imperatives with common or garden morality as we have been discussing it. Indeed in some variants, e.g. Sidgwick's,[5] the high-minded

[4] This is what often causes it to seem "moderate", with which being rational is often equated. But its *free* character is the prior reality.

[5] H. Sidgwick, *The Methods of Ethics*, London 1874.

version turns out to be a matter of acting *as if* one heteronomously acknowledged the sway of ordinary or traditional morality, even though one does not, since this course will be for the best. The same reasoning was used by the atheist acquaintance of G.K. Chesterton's father who carried a Prayer Book with him on his Sunday walk because it set a good example. Though not wishing to appear low-minded by contrast one may yet feel oneself to be on safer ground if one not only insist, *with* these theorists, that there *is* a common and traditional morality (which they, however, consider it the proper business of philosophical ethics to transcend), but even agree with Aristotle, in contrast to them, that such customary beliefs or "norms" constitute the foundational principles of the science of ethics itself.[6] It was a welcome relaxation of this attitude when Alan Donagan effectively demonstrated[7] that ethics had to take into account existing traditinal morality, which he called either Hebrew-Christian or "Orwellian", Kant in any case being seen as the great exponent of it. For Donagan, however, traditional morality was as it were the matter or content for which the philosopher had to discover or supply the form or master-principle upon which the tradition could be critically presented as constituting a system. This would be theory *of* morality and hence also meta-ethical. Thus Donagan too leaves behind that actual, existent morality which is a controlling feature of human life as it is lived and of which, and not of individual philosophical theories of it, we are seeking the origin. Donagan wishes, just as Kant did, to separate ideal reason from existent morality as its judge, providing the latter with an over-arching law in terms of which this reason evaluates possible candidates for the title of moral precept, a two-tier system (corresponding to ethics and "meta-ethics").

In fact, however, the idea or "norm" that one should follow or obey the deliverances of reason (Donagan's master principle) is, in the moral tradition, just one precept among all the others.[8] So much is this so that in the name of *other* moral considerations people such as Blake (*Marriage of Heaven and Hell*) or D.H. Lawrence (*Fantasia of the Unconscious*) have been quite well able to question whether we *ought* to be reasonable. The question makes sense, even if the answer has to be "yes", but on Donagan's scheme there is no coherent possibility of putting the question at all. It is antecedently ruled out by the idea that morality *just is* what reason prescribes, reason itself being somehow preter-moral. This is crucially different from identifying morality

[6] Aristotle, *Ethica Nich. I.*

[7] A. Donagan, *The Theory of Morality*, Chicago 1977.

[8] The *traditional* controlling principle, rather, is that good is to be pursued, evil avoided, i.e. that one is to get into a practical frame of mind, work in pursuit of the end (*bonum*), whatever it may be. Being rational or obeying law is just one of the secondary precepts, the reason why one should act rationally being that intellect is the form of human nature and *thus* or as such will lead man to his natural fulfilment. It is not a constraint as of "pure duty".

with (practical) rationality, where the latter is seen as in reality the principle or "form" of any deliberate human behaviour whatever. For this latter move is metaphysical rather than analytical and definitional. One can still ask whether after all it is morally obligatory to "follow" reason, whether one might not choose to be mad, as in W.B. Yeats's theory of "The Moods", and a reason can be given why not (it deflects from the attainment of the end). But one can't even suggest that reason itself might prescribe that one not follow reason's own prescriptions, unless, that is, one is opting simply to drop out of the game, so to say, to drop the moral stance (seen as one of several stances one might adopt). But then what was the value of such a stance in the first place? That question seems, for such theorists, to be strictly off limits. They have no argument against the "option" of irrationality since they do not connect reason with the rational soul as principle of the whole living being, man.

How the mistake comes to be made is easy to see, and leads us a step further in our enquiry. We asked the question whether we have a particular morality as distinct from the idea itself of morality. Certainly we talk of the particular morality of a given tribe or civilization. But does the human race as a whole have a particular morality? The answer is affirmative in so far as there is a particular moral tradition.

We will not here give the question, or spectre, of moral relativism or pluralism the pride-of-place treatment it has commonly been getting. It was dealt with adequately years ago in what Schörnborn called *un brillant essai*.[9] The flexible approach of Thomas Aquinas to the question has a lot to commend it.[10] But in fact one could, if one wished, treat the corpus of all known moral judgments ever made as Hans Kelsen proposed treating recorded systems of law. Like Donagan one would then come up with a system; one would also be able to show, in accordance with Hume's famous thesis (of no ought from an is), how the more exotic opinions have all been derived in some way from the better known maxims, how some of these have on occasion been stressed to the neglect of others. In short, even on some kind of positivistic account of ethics one can dispose of the relativist hypothesis as both unnecessary and of doubtful sense.[11]

What is certainly true of this human moral tradition, however, is that we are typically acquainted with it in such objectified forms as sacred books, parrotted proverbs, codes of law, socially canonized forms of behaviour and speech. All this suffices to prevent many people from ever even entertaining the idea

[9] C. Schönborn, "*L'homme créé par Dieu: le fondement de la dignité de l'homme*", *Gregorianum* 1984, p.353. The reference is to C.S. Lewis, *The Abolition of Man*, London 1943. Cf. H. Veatch, *Rational Man*, Bloomington 1964, pp.37-46.

[10] Cf. *Summa theologiae Ia-IIae* Q 94, art. 2-6.

[11] Cf. Hugo Meynell, "Doubts about Wittgenstein's Influence", *Philosophy* (London) 1981.

that morality is nothing other than reason or rationality itself (in the conduct of life). Reason, after all, is a faculty, an invisible power of our nature, while morality is a social and historical fact.

Many people, in fact, are inclined to insist that morality is only a part of practical reason, which only *some* of life's situations call into exercise. One can call this attitude moralism.[12] There is of course such a thing as art (*techne*), but even here there is question of how best to practise the art, and that question is moral, i.e. it falls under ethics (even where the art itself, e.g. burglary, is morally objectionable), concerned as it is with attaining our human end, ultimately a matter of how to be happy. We have already seen how this moral or ethical faculty is exercised, cannot fall into abeyance, even during a theoretical discussion of morality itself, and the same would apply during the exercise of any art. The moral, the practical, as concerned with the *actus humanus* as just, is to do with all and any behaviour as perfecting (successfully or unsuccessfully) the agent. Art, though also practical, is concerned with perfecting the work or thing made, the *factibile*, not the *agibile*, even though producing the *factibile* is itself an *agibile*, a human action freely chosen. Thus artists can be, must be, thorough or slovenly in their work, honest or dishonest.

How to be happy, we said. That is *the* moral question, that is the constitutive direction (and directive) of practical reason (as concerned with perfecting the agent himself, whatever he may be materially doing). As directive it is expressed in the precept *bonum est persequendum et malum evitandum*, i.e. follow what leads to the end and avoid what doesn't. This is the formal character of even the bad man's activity; it is how it appears to him, given that he is acting freely. It is the evil of theories of altruism to aspire to separate morality from this primal urge to fulfilment, introducing an eternal discordancy into the heart of man. If one's own joy is not to be fulfilled in the happiness of others, what will ever motivate one to seek this happiness? Some kind of priggishness or worse is bound to step into the vacuum. *Corruptio optimi pessima.*

Notions of altruism are in fact a symptom of an unacceptable individualism which has no theory of man in community. Yet no individual can be perfectly happy as long as *anyone* is miserable, and we need to believe, as far as any possible happiness in its full sense goes, that "all shall be well and all manner of thing shall be well," though we need not profess to know how this shall be so. Mother Julian of Norwich, who uttered the prophecy (c.1343-c.1416), believed, not without some tension, that it was compatible with the eternal misery of the reprobate. In seeking, anyhow, the common good we each seek our own happiness or perfection, so there is no place for altruism as defined against this.

---

[12] Cf. Henry Veatch, "Are there Non-Moral Goods?" *The New Scholasticism*, Autumn 1978.

We said that morality, as a phenomenon, is necessarily found only in the particular concrete traditions, as the genus is only found in the species, and these traditions are best seen as various approximate embodiments of practical reason, of what it prescribes and commands. The traditions, indeed, have taken shape down the ages, though this is not at all to say that reason has taken shape down the ages. Reason, again, is a power of the soul (*potentia animae*), and so wherever there is a (human) soul there is reason. No doubt the operation or actualization of this power requires a certain development of sense-life. We may take it though that with man as man having that power morality has originated, and no doubt a lot of honouring of father or mother went on before someone thought to enunciate a corresponding command. Perhaps, indeed, as with the dogmatic definitions of the Church, it was only enunciated in proportion as it was violated. The principle, as constitutive of reason, was always there.

But then why should such *reason* originate, carrying with it as it were its own title to nobility? Would we not have to say with Cicero that it originated with the divine mind? "Let us make man to our image and likeness." For unless reason is so *guaranteed* then there is no knowledge of morality if morality is taken to name some kind of unconditional claim, but only of human customs having no such claim for "free spirits", such as we are.

Those who stress the hypothetical nature of moral imperatives need not balk at talk of an unconditional claim. For it is surely the great weakness of the categorical imperative theory that it entirely separates considerations of the *purposes* of actions from their phenomenal character as a succession of events. They get their *formal* character, by contrast, from their end or purpose, i.e. this is what specifies them, both naturally and morally, though the moral end may differ from the act's more immediate and natural object. Hence it belongs to the very meaning (ratio) of a precept, too, that it be given for some purpose.[13] Now the unconditional claim of morality bears firstly upon that purpose (the *bonum* sought) and only secondly upon the behaviour which is a means to it, which is thus in *that* sense, i.e. *qua* behaviour, hypothetical.

Now freedom of will is only checked by truth, since outside of truth there is no freedom. But truth only comes to the mind in so far as one can say of anything, it *is* so. We can say this both of states of affairs which we find in being and, differently, of proposed states of affairs the actualization or not of which depends on our choices, our behaviour. Here we judge what *is to be* (though it is still true that it *is so* that such and such is to be). There is no relativizing of the import of "is". Hence it is that the claim to say what anything is makes no sense on a purely immanentist evolutionary scheme. It is out of all proportion, for example, to any possible survival value (though it serves for that as well, of course).

[13] Cf. Aquinas, *Summa theologiae* Ia-IIae 99, 1.

What we need in order to explain or justify morality is a knowing power *constitutive* of what it knows, setting all things in order as Anaxagoras says. It would be the reflected light of that, like an image in a mirror, of which man, confident of his power to reason, would be and in fact is the beneficiary. It gives him the insight both that "all nature is akin" and that "the soul has learned everything",[14] i.e. it has the potentiality of taking the whole of reality for its province, so that there can be nothing real of which it cannot speak, but only a temporary silence while it finds, or gets supplied to it, the right words and thoughts. What binds us to this conception is our inability to discard reason's and hence morality's unconditional claim, as, for example, our recurring anger at, typically, the injustice of others underlines. We are not able to confuse that anger with a mere rage of disappointment.

The origin of morality, it becomes clear, is God. It can *only* be that, as applies equally to human reason as a whole.[15]

[14] Plato, *Meno*.

[15] Aquinas too in this matter (and not only Descartes) uncharacteristically appeals directly to the primary cause, citing Aristotle in further support: "the principle of considering and understanding is some intellective principle higher than our intellect, which is God, as also Aristotle says in VII Ethic. or Mag. mor. chapter XVIII" (*Summa theol.* Ia 82, 4 ad 3um). Of course he is dealing here with the motion (*motus*) of the intellect rather than with its truth, but it is easy to ascertain that he shared the view of Cicero which we cited (from *De Legibus* II, 4, 10) as to how reason can constitute a moral *law*, it being "the light of intellect sown into us (*insitum*) by God" (*De duobus praeceptis caritatis collatio*, see *Opera Omnia*, Parma 1866, Vol. XVI, p.97a).

Chapter 3

The Moral Sphere and the Practical Sphere

Part of the force of our last chapter was to establish that there can be no properly human acts which are morally indifferent when considered specifically as *exercised*. This says no more than that in a technical or artistic performance, for example, it is a human being who carries out the work, and his doing a job cannot be separated from his ongoing activity of self-perfection, though the two aspects are of course distinguishable. He does his work well or badly, also from the moral point of view, and hence, as Aristotle pointed out, if an artist acts against the normal laws of his art he can be a better craftsman if he does it knowingly than if it occurs out of incompetence, even though the opposite is the case where we are thinking of laws of behaviour (of course in the widest sense, which would include, for example, the obligations, real enough, of *epieicheia*: thus a knowing failure to exercise *epieicheia* would *always* be worse than the more usual involuntary legalism). It is in this sense that there is also no "value-free" exercise of scientific research. We never abdicate from our moral responsibility, i.e. it is not within the scope of our freedom to do so since such responsibility results from that rational nature upon which all freedom is based.

The theme deserves further development. We saw in our first chapter how those we might call social engineers suffered from a kind of ethical blindness brought on by the inherited notion criticized here, viz. that ethics or morality only come into play at certain specific points within the wider realm of human activity generally. This is also, of course, the background to notions of *realpolitik*. The wise or effective or even great-souled statesman should not concern himself too much with morality, it is thought, should not mind too much "getting his hands dirty", a metaphor which simply assumes the wrong view of ethics in order to play down its centrality to human endeavour. In fact it is within the science of ethics as understood by Aristotle or Aquinas that one finds treated, in the analysis of, for example, greatness of soul itself, *magnanimitas*, all that can come under the heading of political aspiration. Such a virtue, like any other, on account of the basic unity of the virtues, is incompatible with the simple injustice involved in "getting one's hands dirty" and the harm this does to the common good, inclusive of the good sought by the great-souled man.

Moral theory, we are saying, is an account of man as such, man as an agent, that is, not as a biological phenomenon; of how he is to be (in order to succeed as an agent), what habits he needs, what he is to aim at. Such a nature of course rests upon his biology, i.e. upon those ontological realities of which his rationality forms part. Because of this rationality there is needed a study of man separate from biology[1], and this is the study of him as free, as source of his own actions. This study of him is called ethics, and it includes an account, which may be critical, of how men come to form those customs of behaviour (as distinct from the internal habits of virtue we all need) which we call a society's morality. In so far as these customs are not understood any longer we have to do with a morality in decay. We need to understand why we should act in a certain way, if our actions are not be merely compulsive and less than human and hence morally bad. So we need to understand what we want out of life and how we are to aim at it. It is only in a very restricted sense that we can meaningfully ask what we ought to want; in general the wants come first, particularly the general want or wanting to be *happy*. Since it is not within our freedom to question whether we want this such a question would not fall within the scope of ethics either. Imagining one can raise the question, given that the rational confusions involved in it have been exposed, seems best treated in pathology.

But the notion, the paradigm, of a *special sphere* of the moral, as it were beyond that of "interest", dies hard.[2] It is often taken that we are all agreed that there is such a sphere, which we might choose to deny, thus becoming "amoral", a state sometimes identified with being somehow primitively good, like the young woman in Mervyn Peake's *Mr. Pye*. It turns out, however, that these young women, of whom there are not a few in modern fiction, actually have a deeper morality than the customary one of which they are innocent, thus bearing out our thesis of morality as covering the whole of any possible behaviour. Their ancestor is Mary Magdalen, great saint of love and wastrel of precious ointment.

It might even seem that we cannot do without this idea of a special, restricted sphere in some form, since even after digesting radical criticism of such moralism[3] people will replace it with a fresh version of "the moral motive" as something distinguishable from human striving in general,[4] even though it is just the latter which needs to be ordered and explained, i.e. it is not the business of any true morality (or moral theory) to introduce some sort of secondary constraint upon such striving as such.

---

[1] Even though we grant that his intellect as *forma corporis* is part and parcel of his biology, the workings of which can be studied in psychology. What is studied in ethics is man's responsibility, man as master and *principium* or originator of his own acts, given that he is free in the way that his psycho-biology shows.

[2] I am not seeking here to destroy the classical doctrine of the *bonum honestum*, as I hope will become ever clearer.

[3] E.g. that offered by Anscombe (1958) or Philippa Foot (1970).

[4] E.g. A. Donagan, *op. cit.*

The root factor in the various protestations of loyalty to morality, to *Sittlichkeit*, is a sense of obligation, supposed, despite its transcendence, to attach to only *some* possible human actions. Anscombe had argued that this approach only makes sense within a theistic scheme of things, after which Donagan tried to reinstate it upon non-theistic, Kantian premises.[5] It was only due to this climate of inherited "respect for the law" that writers such as R.M. Hare could assume as obvious that morality was a matter of imperatives, a view successfully refuted by P. Foot[6], who in her later work went on to ditch the notion of obligation altogether.[7]

Regarding imperatives Aquinas, we know, distinguished laws and obligations from imperatives, inasmuch as the judgment, this is to be done(*hoc est faciendum*), differs from the command, do this (*fac hoc*).[8] For Aquinas, all the same, an imperative is in the first place equally an act of reason (*imperare est actus rationis*), not of will as it seems to be for Hare, so that the distinction in itself does not encourage the postulation of a second type of meaning, the "prescriptive". The form of the gerundive judgment, indeed, is the same as that of any predication, viz. S is P, and, in the Latin language at least, could not be otherwise.[9]

Obligations, all the same, are pretty close to imperatives, and if one habitually thinks of one's activities as hemmed in by obligations, rather than as ordered by the patterns of nature, and possibly revelation, together with the corresponding virtues, then it is understandable that one will tend to restrict such obligations to a special class of commanded or forbidden actions. This might seem more tolerable than the idea that reason, as source of *all* our human acts, is itself in essence a transmitter of law and a giver of commands. Law, after all, as coming from a legislator or, like grace, from God, according to Aquinas, is an exterior principle of activity, unlike the powers and habits of the soul, which are intrinsic to man himself.

In this way there will be no morally indifferent acts, though at least some action-types, viewed in the abstract, might seem indifferent. To pay a given sum for a given item is indifferent in the abstract; in the real situation though I have either acted justly or unjustly, along, necessarily, with the engagement of other virtues. As actions engage the virtue of prudence, so action-types engage moral science (*scientia moralis*). Now many authors go on from this to

[5] Cf. Theron, "The Moral Law and Theism", *The Thomist*, January 1983.

[6] P. Foot, "When is a Principle a Moral Principle?" *Aristotelian Society Supplement* XXVIII, 1954.

[7] P. Foot, "Morality and Art", *Proceedings of the British Academy* 56 (1970).

[8] Aquinas, *Summa theol. Ia-IIae* 17, 1.

[9] Hence G. Grisez's postulation of a second type of *copula*, viz. "is to be", seems a wildly mistaken interpretation, actually following the same path as Hare (cf. Theron, *Philosophy or Dialectic?*, Introduction, on this point).

identify *prudentia* with "personal moral reasoning", a somewhat ambiguous phrase. According to V. Bourke, for example, this is "so personal that it can only be performed by the agent faced with his own moral problem; as such it is unique and incommunicable."[10] Taken literally, however, this would mean that no judgment *at all* could be passed upon another person's prudential act, which seems unrealistic. The identical claim was made by Hare at the start of his *Freedom and Reason*,[11] and it controls the whole development of the argument of that profoundly voluntarist book.[12] The claim is open to the charge of confusing judgment and decision. One can hardly deny that one can make a judgment, perform moral reasoning, about another man's moral problem or the "final solution" he comes up with. But of course one cannot make his decision for him.[13]

The prejudice about incommunicability is strong, however. Thus McDowell writes that "one knows what to do... not by applying universal principles but by being a certain kind of person,"[14] as if not noticing that the alternatives are not mutually exclusive. One may know what to do by being specifically the kind of person who does apply universal principles. Of course I must apply them well and here both intellectual and moral virtues are engaged, which is probably what McDowell was thinking of. But one can give a rational and hence communicable account of such virtues.

The term "universal", in fact, does or should do little more than indicate that the principle of intelligible explanation is in place in moral matters. That is, the alternatives facing a human agent can be thought and talked about. *Principles* of action are bound to come into play, action and deliberation being what they are, and the question might be raised, for one used to speaking of *moral* principles or of "values", as to which of these principles are "moral". Philippa Foot's answer to that was that principles are only seen as moral "if we suppose a certain background"[15]. The background, she says, is roughly that "collection of things we call virtues and vices", though as she never explains why we "call" them this we might not seem to have come very far in explaining why some principles are "seen as" moral. Against Hare's stress on universality as morally defining, however, she points out that however general a principle may be we are unable to see it as moral if we cannot "fill in the background" by relating it to just this collection. The collection,

[10] Vernon Bourke, "The Synderesis Rule and Right Reason", *The Monist* 66, No. 1, January 1983.

[11] Oxford 1963, p. 1: "A man who is faced with such a problem knows that it his own problem, and that nobody can answer it for him."

[12] Cf. Theron, *Morals as Founded on Natural Law*, chapter 1 (Frankfurt 1987).

[13] Cp. Aquinas, *QD de veritate*, XVII, 1 ad 4um.

[14] "Virtue and Reason", *The Monist* 1979, pp. 331-350.

[15] See note 6. The "seen as" betrays the limitations operative upon the concerns of "analytical" philosophers.

however, for all Foot tells us, might be no more than a haphazard tradition, though it has at least the merit, as against Hare's "universal prescriptivism" and "meagre concepts", of not being undifferentiated. The word "good", she says, cannot do its work without "honesty", "sincerity", "murder", "stealing", "ostentation", "treachery" and so on, and these are precisely *concepts*, not principles.

> Each expression of this kind carries with it a special way of looking at something, it is wrong to think of these terms as having a descriptive element of their own but an "evaluative" element in common.[16]

If it is a concept rather than a superior principle, a kind of *looking* as when we distinguish an act as one of treachery rather than of laziness, or of prudence, which determines whether some principle is of the moral type, then, she says, "understanding what someone says about what is right and wrong is not like understanding an order." The link with imperatives dissolves.

Instead of connecting evaluation and prescription with willing and being consistent in one's willing[17], as if all value were thus imposed upon a neutral world of "facts", we have to acknowledge that it is how people and the world are which is the natural starting-point for deciding what is to be done.[18] How, indeed, might one be persuaded to confer value upon a "value-free" world unless, in the world, one believed that such conferral would have value, though this contradicts the whole project? We can say, rather, that there is an ordinary grading mechanism, for apples as for human action, for even if apples are more "dispensable" than good actions the *logical* meachanism is the same.[19]

There is a clear kinship of these views with Aquinas's statement that instead of all morals being derived from "Do good and avoid evil" there are in fact several precepts of natural or moral law (depending upon the hierarchy of our natural inclinations[20]). This makes it less plausible to claim that moral goodness is a distinct and separable species of goodness simply considered. Human actions too are good when they are as they should be, like apples. Of course an act may be good in its execution, and yet not a *due* act, and besides considering what acts are due I should perform an act well if I do it at all and, more subjectively, as well as I can. But this applies as much to cricket or theft as to alms-giving, and even while performing an act of theft there are certain moral

---

[16] *Op. cit.* p.108.

[17] This "connection" is really a *reduction* of the ethical, of moral law. Analogously, Luther reduced being saved to believing that one was saved.

[18] Hare himself does this, *quasi veritate coactus*; cf. *op. cit.* p.185: "given that people are as they are and the world as it is" etc.

[19] Cf. J.O. Urmson, "On Grading", *Mind* 1950, cited in Theron, *op. cit.*

[20] I.e. even if they are applications of the first principle their application is not determined by the content of the first principle itself, but by the natural inclinations.

considerations operating, as we saw there are in all the arts, all concern with *factibilia*. This is why St. Thomas says that any act of man could always be worse than it is.

*

* *

We can complete Foot's work of exposing the wrongness of Hare's analysis of the logic of moral discourse. Law is something belonging to reason, not will, says Aquinas, and we have considered some of the arguments for this position. In freeing the notion of a precept (*hoc est faciendum*) from that of a command according to a precept (*fac hoc*) one preserves the rationality of morals and of law in general. One can then understand how thinking can be at once rational and practical, weakness of will needing in itself to play no *dialectical* role.[21]

Thus a precept, such as *bonum est persequendum*, can have obligatory force even if it "does not have the obligatory force of an imperative".[22] The precept that murder is not to be committed, forming, as it does, a part of each man's rational knowledge, obliges him not to murder, all the time. But if it *commanded* him, all the time, i.e. if he commanded himself, not to murder, then, with Hare, we would have to say that if he *did* murder then his reason did not recognize the precept, *whatever he said*.[23] All murderers would be in good faith and the situation of doing what one knows one ought not to do becomes a straight conceptual contradiction, something different from that contradiction in performance which we normally attribute to the knowingly evil act, in which the sinner somehow willingly suspends considerations which ought to have guided him.

We are indeed obliged to follow the prescriptions for making a bomb *if* we want a bomb. What we are *not* obliged to do is to want a bomb. In logically just the same way we are obliged to follow the first precept of natural law, to pursue the good, *if* we want to attain our natural end. It is in this sense that moral "imperatives" can be called hypothetical. But we are absolutely obliged to want to attain our natural end itself, at least under pain of not attaining it, which is absolute enough. It is in this sense that Aquinas sees the *ends* of actions as primarily obligatory, and here we should remember that such ends are ontologically intrinsic to the actions themselves[24], so that there is only an

[21] Cf. Theron, *The Recovery of Purpose*, Frankfurt 1994, chapter 6.

[22] Bourke, *op. cit.* p.71.

[23] Hare, *op. cit.* p.83, "he thinks that he thinks he ought, but he has escaped his own notice using *ought* in an off-colour way." The view of course assumes that to command myself to act *is* to will myself to act, while for Aquinas the will can go contrary to the command (*imperium*) of reason.

[24] All the same, we have to distinguish the natural end or *object* of a given type of act from the moral end which may happen (*accidit*) to it in practice, thus specifying it morally, even though this moral end and the natural end (object) often coincide while, indeed, the act's natural

appearance of the hypothetical. It is this imposition of *ends* which is distinctive of natural law theory and which clashes with any notion of morality as in the service of some personally elected "plan of life".

There is no reason why the ends of action should not be obligatory. The obligation is expressible in the same form, viz. this end (*bonum*) is to be worked towards, being backed up by the more general obligation to pursue some end or other, to act rationally, to live. To deny that such a general obligation is moral is a first step towards condoning suicide. But we are to have ends, reason is to be practical, tendencies (of the natural inclinations) are to be followed.[25]

*

* *

The moral sphere then, the sphere over which moral or practical principles operate, extends over the whole of human praxis, if we allow that the intellectual, but practical, virtue of *art* is never *exercised* without such exercise being controlled by the *moral* virtues (as distinct from the intellectual virtues) of industry, truthfulness and so on, as well perhaps as by the three theological virtues.[26] Here the concept of right reason (*recta ratio, orthos logos*) emerges, of reason that is practical in so far as it is ordained to activity or, better, to production, both of actions and of technical products (*agibilia* and *factibilia*). The principles of *praxis* constitute the corpus of moral principles, of the natural law, that is to say. It follows, again, that it is reason that legislates.

Reason, however, is not itself, of course, the set of precepts which it legislates. The term "morality", as referring to this set of precepts, stands and "stood for a standard by which systems of mores, actual and possible, were to be judged and by which everybody ought to live, no matter what the mores of his neighbour might be."[27]

The notion of a standard, however, complexifies under analysis. What sort of an entity is it, if it is real at all? Donagan speaks of the Stoics as *forming* "the first reasonably clear conception of morality", of this standard. Strictly, one assumes that they formed this standard on the evidence of their having *formulated* it. But they must have formed this (theoretical) conception while

object may set limits to what legitimate other moral ends there can be to it. One may not pervert our nature for the sake of a good end, may not murder to save life.

[25] Followed, not imposed. See our *Philosophy or Dialectic?* (Frankfurt 1995), "Introduction: Metaphysics, Dialectic and the Human Task", for a critique of G. Grisez's exposition of this point.

[26] This raises the general question, belonging to theology, of whether the moral virtues concerned would be infused or acquired or both, which we need here do no more than mention.

[27] Donagan, *op. cit.*

reflecting upon the standard as already operative in their practical reasoning. Hence they claimed that there *is*, and was before them, a morality valid for all men in virtue of their common rationality, whether or not anyone had "formed a conception of it". The same would apply to logic before Aristotle, or as followed by those who never read Aristotle. It is this abiding datum of reason, this standard, that a theory of morality is a theory of.

The Stoics or their predecessors, then, must have had an unclear conception all along, which was not the standard but *of* it. This, that they possessed, might be described as an innate capacity or potentiality to form the later, clearer capacity (as St. Thomas refers to the intellect as *capax Dei*, while Aristotle speaks of it as "in some way all things" or everything). Such a capacity may not be fully or clearly exercised for centuries. But insofar as it is innate, as a capacity, we will have to grant that the mind is not absolutely *tabula rasa*. It has a certain *nature*, such that it will form just this standard, no doubt as a faithful mirroring in its own mode of the requirements of practical human reality. That is, all knowledge comes from the senses indeed, but it is the determinate *spiritual* nature of mind which determines that this will indeed be knowledge. As Aquinas says, "the principles of intellectual cognition are naturally known."[28] Thus the standards of logic are not innate as formulated, but an actual having of the particular power to formulate them under normal human conditions is innate. The same applies to practical reason, though it is in some respects an analogy that is operative here insofar as the principles of logic are also employed in practical thinking, whereas the reverse is not the case. Practical and theoretical reason are not parallel powers, but the former is an extension of the latter.[29]

Now does the identification of the moral standard with the first principles of practical reason amount to a full *justification* of this standard? This would imply that it was sufficient for justifying behaviour that one said of it that it was reasonable. In many contexts this is indeed so, but one can wish to question reason and the need to be reasonable, particularly if reason has come to be viewed as hostile to the vital impulse, for example. A philosophical explanation which made it formally impossible to raise the question of reason's credentials would, therefore, not be a complete explanation.[30]

Unfortunately this seems to be true of Donagan's explanation, his "theory of morality". According to him "common morality" consists of apparently theoretical judgments "that actions of certain kinds are unconditionally contrary to reason, and hence cannot be performed by a human being inasmuch as

[28] *Summa theol. Ia-IIae* 10, 1.

[29] This plainly Thomistic doctrine has often been forgotten by those interpreting Ia-IIae 94, 2, of the *Summa theologica*.

[30] This was really the point at issue between C.S. Lewis and G.E.M. Anscombe about "naturalism".

he is rational."[31] Acting contrary to reason, however, is just one of the kinds of action which morality forbids. Reason, indeed, as expressive of intellect, is the highest, most formal part of our nature, but it is not our whole nature, and so morality also forbids other unnatural acts, such as bestiality or sodomy; certainly this is so if we are speaking, with Donagan, of traditional morality. Now these acts are not wrong because they are contrary to reason, even though they are that. They are wrong as contrary to our animal, generic nature, as an abuse of it. Even if this were not so it could be so. Lying, again, is first of all more of an abuse of the speech faculty than of reason itself. It is the more routine acts of injustice or intemperance, of imprudence or lack of due fortitude which seem more directly and specifically against reason. Similarly in a system of law one has to admit that the law that law is to be obeyed is no different in form from the law that murder is not to be done. They are equally "acts of practical reason", as is the law or verdict that actions contrary to reason are not to be performed. It is in no way a master law, at a higher remove from other laws. So one cannot set it over against them so as to motivate a codification of them. Hence it is not the case that each law or act of practical reason *states that* practical reason prescribes its content. Each law is merely such a prescription.

Why should reason not prescribe that reason is to be obeyed? Of course the general problem then arises that it is only in virtue of one of the laws within the system that we are bound to obey all the others. In fact though we have seen that this is not entirely so. Even though reason forbids all wrong acts this wrongness is not identical with irrationality. Some wrong acts, and hence some irrational acts, are wrong for other reasons.

It would be much more compelling and "complete" if there stood over against the system a "general form of reason" or something similar which was self-validating and such that there was no need for the law that reason is to be obeyed. Or if we could *presuppose* that when reason prescribes, say, that every rational being is to be respected it "functions without error". But nothing is plainer than that we cannot merely presuppose that conscience gives the right advice[32] or that it is not, rather, just this way of deciding things that stifles achievement of what is desired. It has to be shown. This is not of course to say that it has to be shown before anyone can be morally justified in following conscience. But it has to be shown before one can claim to have justified *a theory of* morality on rational foundations.

*

* *

[31] *Op. cit.* p.53.
[32] Cf. P.H. Nowell-Smith, *Ethics*, London 1954, ch.18, "Conscience".

On the classical theory the precepts of natural law are supplied by the inclinations of our shared generic nature. Just as the common good is in part identical with each person's own good, inasmuch as, for example, he harms his own good when he harms the common good, so, analogously, the personal dictate of prudence in the concrete situation should not be conceived of as other than the natural law. As St. Thomas says, the natural law can be added to (by reason), but never subtracted from, and there is no reason why wise decisions made in concrete situations should not be viewed as additions to natural law, in the sense of supplying precedents for the future.[33]

We might say with the youthful Fuchs that "the spiritual encounter of man with his own being… is in fact an encounter with God," the law-giver. "The demand of the natural law of this moment is a personal appeal made directly by God to me… In the light of such personal understanding of reality and the natural law, it becomes more evident that the doctrine of the absolute validity of the natural law in no way contradicts the statement that God appeals to the individual and gives his commands in an individual and personal manner."[34]

That is, the difference between moral philosophy, let us say, and moral or prudential reasoning is not so clearcut as some would make out. Personal responsibility is indeed incommunicable, but the conditions for that responsibility may be the same for everyone, as the common things can be the most deeply loved.

Philosophy of course includes the so-called meta-ethical, that which is clearly theoretical, not practical at all. But moral philosophy or ethics also and principally includes the attempt to say in universal terms (*scientia est de universali*) what should be done. Conversely, at least a large part of prudence is concerned with recognizing instances of these universal and canonized judgments. Hence one says that the divine knowledge itself subsumes all these particular situations under universal prescriptions. But if this is possible for an infinite mind then human prudence can be thought of rather as reason working with rapid intuition in situations not granting time or ability to explicate them theoretically, rather than as a second *type* of thinking which is "incommunicable". Thus epieicheia or equity, the virtue of knowing when to break the law, is itself treated by Aquinas as a general virtue like all the others. Significantly, he sees it as a part not of prudence but of justice.

I once heard someone say, "I was a pacifist until 1940, then it didn't seem possible to be a pacifist any more." This by no means would show that certain factors in 1940 were unamenable to those mental universalizing processes

---

33 Cf. J. Walgrave, "Reason and Will in Natural Law", in *Lex et Libertas* (ed. Elders & Hedwig), Vatican 1987.

34 J. Fuchs, *Natural Law*, Dublin 1965, pp.132-133. For our purpose here we need only grant the *possibility* of this scenario. Still, the theistic perspective is needed to make sense of moral obligation in the first place.

which had led the man to pacifism. Rather, confronted with them, he saw that pacifism was the wrong or an incomplete response (i.e. if his later judgment was correct), saw that his previous reasoning had been defective, whether or not he took time to sit down and try to work out just how this was so.[35]

It follows that even though studying ethics is no large part of virtue it can and should be part of the virtuous life as opportunity permits. The professor's ethics are not of a different kind, he just has more time to devote to them. Nor is it true that his deliberations have no natural issue in action. To work out a positive justification for humility is to motivate oneself to live humbly. Nor is he unique in often finding himself theorizing about situations in which he is not himself placed. This is always a remote preparation for a future eventuality, even if that of merely being called on to give advice. Neither does systematization militate against these considerations. We find an analogous situation where people want to make all metaphysics the preserve of the professors, as if, for example, the creative artist had no metaphysical mission.

So the claim includes a conviction that whenever one even merely *thinks* about doing any action, even writing this chapter, one is acting according to natural law. One's action has a moral aspect, reflecting the eternal law and the divine image in man, in Aquinas's or Augustine's conception. So much is involved in the concept of a human act. The breadth of this conception is further illustrated by the fact that natural law is never frontally or totally disobeyed, even in the gravest sin. This is not because the sin is not so grave after all, but because natural law is so comprehensive. "Evil is not primarily explained as disobedience to law but as unsuitability of action to end."[36]

---

[35] As McInerny says about moral science and prudential reasoning, "It could be argued that there is not so much a neat break here as a kind of spectrum" (*Ethica Thomistica*, Washington 1982, p.103). Hence any "particular" situation engaging prudence becomes "universal" once one sets about describing it. What makes whatever difference there is, however, is just the remainder which *cannot* be described, the part where music or rhetorical suggestion has to take over, or what Aquinas would call the basic irrationality of matter. What has to be shown, however, is how this confessedly irrational part can make a difference to the ethical judgment, e.g. how the particular quality of the beauty of a given beloved can justify the elopement. Traditionally, we see such factors as affecting culpability rather than as dispensing from the law, still less as restricting its field of application. Reason, we say, must rule the passions. This stricter view, however, in fact requires a more friendly notion of reason itself, as *forma corporis*, than is usual in our post-Calvinist culture.

[36] Aquinas, *Comm. in Sent.* bk. 4, d.33, q.1, 1c.

Chapter 4

Practical Science and Practical Knowledge

We need to explore further the differences between prudential reasoning and ethical studies. We shall pay special attention in this connection to the thought of Aquinas, for whom, as for Aristotle, it was a general feature of a science that it be built out of general or universal principles. *Scientia non est singularium*. The examination of and pronouncement upon particulars as such has no place in science. This was why history, for Aristotle, was not a science, a judgment which the impossibility of separating history from historiography might seem to confirm.

A second requirement for a science, for Aristotle and Aquinas, is that its first principles be either self-evident or capable of being grounded by principles or axioms of a superior science. Otherwise what we have is not knowledge (*scientia*).[1] One should bear this in mind when noting that Aquinas, following Aristotle, teaches that the first principles of ethical science are supplied by human custom (*consuetudo*), this customariness being equivalent, it might seem, to the required self-evidence.[2]

For Aquinas indeed, more clearly than for Aristotle, this conception is illuminated by a doctrine of natural law according to which human nature does not only *de facto* ground a constant issuing into a stable pattern of customs. For Aristotle this often seems to be sufficient for the justification of moral principles. As Gilson remarks:

> The social factor is so important that in his (sc. Aristotle's) eyes the wicked are distinguished from the good, as those who can be kept from evil-doing by *fear* are distinguished from those who can be kept from it by *shame*, or *modesty*.[3]

In a Christian perspective this looks like an idolization of "human respect", and it is perhaps the religious absolutization of ethics which led Western man to take the analysis yet deeper. In any event Aquinas does not stop at the merely *de facto* constant of custom but shows why, and how, these customs can

---

[1] Aquinas, *Summa theol. Ia*, Q1, art. 2.

[2] Behind this lies a theory of induction from experience according to which what we customarily abstract (*epagoge*) from reality would indeed be self-evident, in some degree at least. See Aristotle *Eth. Nic.* I and Aquinas's Commentary I, lect. XI. Cf. *Summa theol.* Ia-IIae 92, 2.

[3] E. Gilson, *The Spirit of Medieval Philosophy*, New York 1940, ch. XVI, note 1. See *Eth. Nic.* X, 10, 1179b 11.

be the first principles of a theoretical science, even if the aim remain action or praxis. When not merely commenting on Aristotle's text he adumbrates his own theory of natural law, built upon theological and Stoic tradition, according to which such law, like reason as a whole, is characterized as a participation in the eternal truth (*lex aeterna*, i.e. God himself in the role of governor of creation) or in the divine light, i.e. in the knowledge which is not ordered by but itself orders all things.[4] On such a view the customs of human society represent the privileged insight of human reason into eternal truths and virtues. At the same time Aquinas takes account of the more pragmatic, even antinomasian Aristotelian solutions, often though ever so subtly shifting the perspective in a way compatible with the more absolutist, Christian approach. Thus he states more firmly than Aristotle that in order to live well it is necessary to know the true end of human life.

Even, then, if custom supplies the first principles of moral science, yet we should not and cannot think that custom supplies the first principles of natural law. These are supplied by *synderesis*, the ineradicable though not actually innate habit of the first practical principles, analogous merely to the inalienable first principles of speculative thought, such as that of non-contradiction and so. The intellect learns these things from the earliest experiences of the senses and it never forgets them. It is in fact the senses which deliver such knowledge to the intellect, though the senses do not themselves understand it. *Et sensus quaedam ratio est*. So these principles are both necessary and *a posteriori*.[5]

So while custom provides the first principles of a natural law ethics a natural *habit* supplies the first principles of (any) praxis. The customs of society, in other words, are so many shorthand and imperfect summations of how man is, of his natural being. Hence the two sets of principles must to some extent coincide. In a similar way the first principles of theoretical science, especially of logic, are also, as self-evident, the first principles of ordinary personal thinking. For thinking is always an activity of *this* person, as is any moral reasoning governed by prudence.

But what corresponds to prudence, then, in theoretical thinking? Well, there are indeed virtues of the theoretical intellect (prudence is both a *moral* virtue, i.e. it is in the will, and also a virtue of the *practical* intellect), viz. *scientia*, science, *intellectus*, understanding and *sapientia*, wisdom.[6] In the case of prudence we seem to have a virtue which is part of practice, of the exercised act, but not of the act as specified in the theoretico-practical science of ethics. Prudence is

---

[4] *Summa theol. Ia-IIae* 91, 2.

[5] Aristotle, *Post. An.* II 19; Aquinas, *Summa theol.* Ia 79, 12, *QD de anima IV ad 6um: Etiam ipsa principia indemonstrabilia cognoscimus abstrahendo a singularibus.*

[6] *Summa theol.*Ia-IIae 57, 2.

concerned precisely, that is to say, with *agibilia*, with things to be done. Thus "someone instructed in moral science could make judgments about acts of virtue even if he himself had no virtue."[7]

The explanation of this might be the presence of the *will* in all activity of the person, but assuredly not in any *scientia*, speculative or practical. This difference, however, of the engagement of will, does not apply to the specifically intellectual virtues, which as exercised are different, also they, from any science.

One should note that the venerable but nonetheless somewhat *ad hoc* distinction between speculative and practical reasoning should not be taken in the sense of a separation, as if the concrete man switches over to a different faculty whenever his speculations take a practical turn. We have only one intellectual faculty, which merely becomes practical by extension at times. Conversely, it is not only the practical intellect which operates, or is *operativus*. "The speculative habit is ordered to an inner work (*opus*) of the intellect, which is to behold the truth."[8] Thus Aristotle had himself said that study is the highest praxis.

Pursuing this matter of the differentiation of theoretical science from informal or intuitive personal speculation, we might seek for a special (intellectual) virtue *of exercise*, playing a role similar to prudence in distinguishing moral thinking from ethical science. There are two types of judgment (*iudicium*), we find St. Thomas claiming, in answer to an objection that theology cannot be wisdom (*sapientia*), as he wants to say, because it is acquired by study, whereas wisdom is a gift (of the Holy Spirit). One kind of judgment is by means of a kind of connaturality with the subject matter (*per modum inclinationis* or *connaturalitatis* or *compassionis*).[9] His example here (it is only that) is that of virtue, "just as one who has the habit of virtue judges rightly concerning those things which are to be done according to virtue inasmuch as he is inclined to them." The other kind of judgment, reasoning from premises to conclusion, he calls the perfect use of reason.[10] In both cases *sapientia* is involved, just as prudence can also be of help in the practice of ethical science.

If we now return to "practical science", then we might seem to have moral science on the one hand, the prudence of the man of good *will* on the other, a prudence inclusive of promptness in the execution of good or mandatory deeds.

---

[7] *Ibid.* Ia 1, 6 ad 3um.

[8] *Ibid.* Ia-IIae 57, 1 ad 1um.

[9] Cf. *Summa theol.* IIa-IIae 45, 2.

[10] *Scientia*, as opposed to *sapientia*, is a use of reason not belonging specifically to a wise man (*iudicium ad sapientem pertineat*), since it is a virtue within a specialization instead of a knowledge of the highest and most general causes, as is *sapientia*. Of this too there is a type which has this character of connatural inclination rather than being of the more plodding, studious kind. This would correspond to what we call *genius*.

There is however a third possibility which one might consider. This would be that of an exact mirroring of the "scientific" situation at the personal level, i.e. without the intervention of the will or of any kind of decision-making, a speculative excogitation of duty according to rules supplied by meta-ethicists (or, at times, ethicists). Much of what we call casuistry would have fallen under this third head.

This latter approach would seem to involve a failure to take account of *electio*, or even a failure to practise it in so far as we are referring to an actual attitude of mind when confronted with a need for moral decision. *Electio*, i.e. choice, called the or an *appetitus praeconsiliati*, a desire for what has been arrived at in deliberation, should follow naturally upon the *consilium* of prudence, since "the merit of prudence does not consist in consideration alone, but in that application to action which is the aim of practical reason,"[11] in which alone prudence consists as being concerned with *agibilia*.[12]

Viewed thus prudence, a virtue or habit, differs totally from conscience, an act, in the view of Aquinas. Not only is conscience a personal intellectual act, but it also differs from prudence in being an act of the *speculative* intellect (which is why we can without contradiction disregard it), though not of course of any science, since by such an act the intellect judges of individual actions performed or to be performed.[13] By conscience too we can judge in either of the two ways, by the connaturality of the virtuous man or by a perfect use of reason possible to good and bad alike. Conscience speculatively applies the first principles of practical reason (held by *synderesis*) in order *truly* to judge a performed or proposed action as good or bad. Hence on the one hand conscience can be erroneous, while on the other we can act against conscience, whether it be correct or in error, since the act of conscience itself, as speculative, is not *directing* us to action.[14]

In contemporary ethics we often have a theory of moral language but no practical or moral science. Instead we are offered a version of personal prudential reasoning based upon no *moral* principles at all, except where they are smuggled in unacknowledged. Yet we seem now to learn that even in Aquinas the *knowledge* of right and wrong need not be practical. What happens then to our notion of a practical science? It might seem largely to be a matter of intention.[15] Thus, for example, of theology as a whole, which Scotus was to declare

---

[11] Cf. *Summa theol.* IIa-IIae 47, 1 ad 3um.

[12] *Ibid.* art.2.

[13] Cf. L.J. Elders, "St. Thomas Aquinas' Doctrine of Conscience", in *Lex et Libertas*, Vatican City 1987.

[14] Cf. Aquinas, *QD de veritate* 17, 1. It seems to me the great failing of R.M. Hare's moral theory not to have acknowledged this.

[15] Cf. J. Maritain, *An Introduction to Philosophy*, Westminster Md. 1991, p. 190: "The division of philosophy into *speculative* and *practical* depends, not on the specific character of the

to be a practical science[16], Aquinas said that it was *more* speculative than practical.[17] Yet if something can be subject to more and less then the difference is not absolute.

So practical science, we see, is not practical in quite the same way as a personal prudential verdict (even in the latter case choice of the will is only *attributed* to prudence, in consequence of its directing such a choice through counsel[18]). Still, and conversely, personal prudence wholly participates in genuine moral science, since this too, as practical, is certainly intended to direct *consilium*. This is so even though, we saw, moral science can exist as a perfect use of reason in a rather vicious professor, whereas prudence would be *intrinsically* flawed if it existed in consideration alone (*sola in consideratione*). The vicious moral professor, possibly futile as a man, may *qua* moral philosopher be successful and good. Yet the goodness of prudence, as a virtue, is inseparable from the goodness of the man. Yet both the science and the virtue are practical inasmuch as they both have a practical end and also because they are both *circa contingentia*, about contingent things such as human actions.[19]

Here might be the place to consider Aquinas's doctrine of law as directive of human actions yet belonging to reason alone. In fact there is a parallel between the use of particular judgments of prudence as models for future decisions and the praxis of jurisprudence. Indeed in so far as the whole knowledge of natural law is *a posteriori* it is difficult to separate it from this kind of accumulation, unless one grants that in one act of *epagoge* one can truly abstract the universal nature present there in reality, of adultery, murder, temperance or justice. But if one can so grasp it from the first, and in one instance, and not merely by trial and error (inadmissible in moral contexts), then is not the difference merely that the moral quality of a given particular act, which prudence might isolate, lacks a name? Thus one could argue that the most individual judgments belong to natural law as much as do general rules.[20] But if we concede so much then it would seem odd not to concede as well that the mind genuinely traces the real skeleton of the body of moral judgment and records this in moral science.

In this connection Vernon Bourke, again, draws attention to the incommunicably personal quality of prudence in Thomas Aquinas, due to the uncertain

---

various philosophic sciences, but on the end which they pursue. If that end is knowledge alone, the philosophy is speculative; if the good of man, it is practical" (See St. Thomas, *Sup. Boet. de Trin.*, q.5 ad 4).

[16] J. Duns Scotus, *Ordinatio Prol.* Pars 5, q.1-2, *De theologia quatenus scientia practica.*

[17] *Summa theol.* Ia 1, 4.

[18] *Ibid.* IIa-IIae 47, 1 ad 2um.

[19] Cf. *ibid.* Ia-IIae 57, 5 ad 3um.

[20] Cf. J. Walgrave, *op. cit.*

and mutable character of the contingent *materia* involved.[21] "Judgment of particular actions is left to the prudence of each person."[22] *Scientia moralis* indeed is "directed to action (i.e. practical), still that action is not the act of the *scientia* but rather of virtue."[23] *Scientia moralis* is concerned with practical actions as "universal species, not as particular acts." So a science is practical by being *directed* to action; prudence, or *recta ratio circa agibilia*, is practical by actually issuing in action.

In support of his point Bourke comments that this personal "prudential discourse cannot be taught to others, although people may be helped to acquire prudential skill by learning from the example and advice of others and by attempts to describe the habit of prudence in universal terms." These attempts are made in ethics, and so we have here a description of the practical function of this practical science. We should note though that what it is said to help one to acquire is a *skill*. Hence Bourke objects to a concept of "practical reasonableness" (J. Finnis) which would cover both moral philosophy and personal decision-making, the third alternative which we mentioned above. This confused notion is connected with a loss of an understanding of practical reason as both truly practical (a skill) and truly reasonable, as well as of the principle, or rather the truth, of analogy.

Aristotle's practical syllogism, having for conclusion an *action*, was thus only analogously a syllogism. "It is not similar in everything... for conclusions are differently related (to the premises) in necessary and in contingent matter."[24] Again, "those things which belong to practical knowledge are perfected in the concrete case... for the end of the practical is action, which has to do with individual realities."[25]

Now there is no *skill* in knowing one's moral science and merely identifying particular situations as falling under one or other of its principles. As André de Muralt says, all radical spontaneity of the will is excluded by such a picture of moral living, a development which he associates with later Thomist commentators such as Capreolus and which, he says, "herald(s) the characteristic structure of modern moral philosophy."[26]

He complains of "a rationalization of the moral act... by substitution of a principle of rational order for the final principle of the voluntary moral act." Freedom is lacking. For Aristotle or Aquinas, though, "voluntary activity

---

[21] V. Bourke, *art. cit.* Cf. S. Theron, "St. Thomas Aquinas and epieicheia", in *Lex et Libertas* (ed. Elders & Hedwig), Vatican City 1987, for possible differences between Aquinas and Aristotle concerning *materia* in morals.

[22] Cf. Aquinas, *In II Eth. Nic.* lect. 2, no. 259.

[23] Cf. Aquinas, *In Boethii de Trinitate* q.V, 1 ad 3um.

[24] Aquinas, *QD de malo*, II, 6 ad 13.

[25] *Contra gentes* III 75.

[26] A. de Muralt, "The *Founded Act* and the Apperception of Others" in *The Self and Others* (ed. Tymeniecka), Dordrecht 1977.

would be specific and autonomous, the good recognized by the intellect being precisely the good that the will seeks as its own real and concrete end, because the will would experience in the natural reality of its spontaneous appetite the coincidence between the natural exigencies of its potency and the end proposed to it by the intellect. In this case, freedom would be the habitual mode of its operation."

No doubt this would be helped on by those attempts to learn from moral science more about those natural aspirations, yet the moral agent is not as such a moral scientist (and nor is moral science theoretical or meta-ethical). It is a question of the relation of precept to inclination. In fact the order of the inclinations of our nature, for Aquinas, simply *is* the order of the precepts of natural law and ethics is in this sense really a matter of doing what one most deeply wants.[27] The modern notion of "moral values", to which one can make an intellectual "passage" (Finnis) from one's inclinations, excludes this.

[27] Cf. H. McCabe, *Law, Love and Language*, London 1968, p.61.

Chapter 5

The Justification of Moral Claims

Opposed to the line of argument which we have been pursuing, with its appeal to custom as representing the repeated response of a stable human nature, seen as itself the only possible source of practical principles, we find a whole industry which is pleased to call itself *meta-ethics*, an of course perfectly legitimate term in itself. Typical, however, of its practitioners is a methodology which binds itself to take no account of actual, generally accepted moral preferences, an attitude of which we found what seemed, in its own way, to be sound criticism in Philippa Foot's writings but one which can be found defended in such classical works as Henry Sidgwick's *The Methods of Ethics*, where the author bases himself on the basic rules of the Enlightenment approach to philosophy and to "scientific method" generally. We will be devoting further space here and in following chapters to our view that such an approach is not sufficient for a philosophical elucidation of morals, for a metaphysics of morals as Kant put it. In order, however, to allow our case to appear in the strongest light we shall be using in many respects methods of just the type which we wish to conclude are inappropriate for ethics.

There is of course a certain kinship, a causal relationship indeed, between such an approach and the formal approach to linguistic usage not only foreshadowed but controlled throughout by Hume's putative discovery of a *naturalistic fallacy*, viz. the fallacy, of a purely logical type, of deriving duties from facts. From our point of view this employment of the tools of the other side, so to say, has the added advantage of focussing this first part of the enquiry upon the *formal* aspect of moral precepts *qua* precepts, *qua* obligations and duties. This, as Maritain points out,[1] is how morality is first experienced by us, and in his presentation of the Thomist outlook the latter appears as in some ways more nearly related to this formally deontological approach of the analysts, typified by Von Wright's "deontic logic", than it might be related to utilitarianism, despite the teleological features which the latter shares with Thomism. Maritain does not seem to share the view, popular among British and American Thomists, that "the utilitarian is the natural ally of the Christian" (i.e. as against Kantian secularist altruism) and it will be interesting in due course to go into why he does not share it, and whether he is right on this point.[2]

*

* *

[1] *An Introduction to the Basic Problems of Moral Philosophy*, Albany 1990, chapters 1 - 3.

[2] His view, indeed, is more differentiated and finely thought out. He writes: "The most appropriate name for Christian morality is not the ethics of happiness, not the ethics of duty in

We might say straight off that if it is granted that the *notion* of morality is a notion always connected with that of practical life then it follows that any moral talk or analysis will have a practical *reference* beyond the internal relations of its concepts to one another. In this way it cannot be assimilated to the idealist view of theoretical thinking as being nothing but the investigation of the relations of our ideas or "representations" with one another. There is necessarily an *object* of moral reference, of which indeed some general theory is desirable, a theory of human actions, for example, or a psychology or, more fundamentally, an anthropology. A mere theory of the *meanings* of moral terms, in other words, is not a sufficient theory of morals. Morality is conditioned by the real object to which its practice is referred.

We can apply this principle of the referential character of moral thought and language by instigating a search for the reference of the word "good", noting in passing that this distinction between meaning and reference[3] saves us from the false idea that moral *language* must be adaptable to changing moral standards (in a given place) in real life. In fact if two references of "good" at two times or places contradict one another then it follows that one of the speakers has made an incorrect reference, in the sense of referring or attributing "good" to something that is not good. For we do not suppose that two conflicting *meanings* are involved.

Some such supposition, however, and perplexity about it, seems to lie behind the assertion that "X is good" can only be a general formula of commendation, as if no one could call a bad thing good, i.e. if he only *means* to commend (one may commend anything and everything). By this procedure it is denied that "good" has a meaning[4] because it is believed that no one meaning emerges from the various uses.

If "X is good" said *nothing* about X except that the present speaker commended it then it would be in principle impossible to envisage grounds for or even to understand the force of such a commendation. For any explanation one

---

the Kantian sense, it is rather the ethics of the honourable good (the ethics of values which are good in themselves and rationally founded), centred on the transcendent and supremely loved good. In this love of the transcendent Good, my own good is involved, to be sure..." (*op. cit.* p.23). He refers to "the happiness friendship brings me — though in a secondary way... which envelops at one and the same time the total fulfilment of my capacities for desire, as a secondary term, and as a primaray term, the transforming union with Another..." Elsewhere he refers to Kant's system as "a perverted Christian moral philosophy" (p.2). Cp. Theron, *Morals as Founded on Natural Law*, p.183.

[3] Aquinas characterized it more correctly as a distinction between *significatio secundum rationem* and *significatio secundum rem*. Both meaning and reference are types of *significatio*, which really means meaning. This insight became blurred in much of the later supposition theory.

[4] Postulating a second category of prescriptive *meaning* is a linguistic device for obscuring this denial (one does of course speak prescriptively at times: the novelty lies in postulating a corresponding subspecies of meaning).

might give could only be in terms of another quality reckoned to be good, and if that predication of goodness in turn said nothing about the quality it was used to commend then no reason would have been given or ever could be given as to why X was good. This not only destroys the notion of goodness but destroys the notion of commendation as well and is therefore self-refuting.

So even if there were no such qualities the moral quality words would still refer to them, or, better, would still *intend* them, as "Pegasus" intends a winged horse, normally understood as an *ens rationis* but which a child might use as he uses "Father Christmas". There is no viable programme for reducing "Father Christmas" to something analogous to a term of pure commendation. The term has to intend a putatively real being. So even if everyone who ever predicates "is good" of a thing approves or commends it, which is by no means certain, yet this cannot be the *meaning* of such a predicate.

One should enquire, all the same, as to why, on any showing, goodness and approval are so closely connected, goodness, which we are now taking as a real quality, seeming to be the ultimate and hence indispensable ground for approval. To identify them would be to take away this essential ground.

If indeed we in any given case approve whatever we do approve on account of some one or more property or other then it is to be expected that these properties themselves have some secondary property in common of a type giving unity and intelligibility to the activity of approving.[5] Thus everything seen is coloured, and just as there are coloured things which have not been seen so there are good things, for example at the bottom of the ocean or in forgotten histories, of which no one has yet approved. This is as certain as the generally accepted view that anyone can expect that he holds some false beliefs.

Approval, after all, does not occur in a mental vacuum. Typically it is a consequence of a judgment or series of judgments which always terminate in the judgment that the thing to be approved is good. Thus "X is good" is often asserted in defence of an approval which we have manifested but are not morally at ease about, and here it may well be used in a misleading way, perhaps prescinding from the more doubtful aspects of the complex in question. It is anyhow made as a statement of fact in order to elicit an act of voluntary evaluation such as approval constitutes. This underlines the fact that in the judgment "X is good" there is no overt commitment of a mentioned subject, such as in "I approve X". There thus seems no final reason to deny that one can judge that something is good without committing oneself to approval, as when one says that it would be good to do X, but one would "rather not". R.M. Hare just begs the question by saying that one is then "using language in

[5] Here one must move beyond a Wittgensteinian theory of focal meaning to an account of analogical concepts corresponding to really analogous properties, properties, that is, allowing for the real individuality of each occurrence, since there is no likeness without difference.

an off-colour way". The situation differs little from that where one says "I know I should have done it, but I just didn't feel like it." One knew, perhaps, that one should have approved of something, or praised a good child, say.

In elucidation of these matters one notes that we naturally prefer to make the assumption or, in our own case, claim that we act out of good will, mean well, though this is of course also the commonest excuse for error. We therefore tend to situate the typical moral conflict in the passage from approving an action to deciding to perform it (and hence performing it), since this, even though the good will be granted, may require some effort ("the spirit is willing but the flesh is weak"). But it is highly probable that the spirit is not *always* willing, or that not all spirits are willing to even approve the good, before the struggle with human weakness even begins. Of course they make *their* good some evil (i.e. some moral evil: no being is ontologically evil), but this cannot imply that the actual good of which they, through malice perhaps, fail to approve thereby changes its meaning in their mouths, becomes the name of some mere moral convention (so that they too cannot speak of it, or "use language in an off-colour way"). Thus my envious neighbour disapproves of my good fortune precisely because he knows that it is good, and the "sour grapes" option, of denying the goodness of goods that one can't have (so that one would only continue to call them good by intentionally "using language in an off-colour way"), is only one of the options open to the envious.

In failing to approve the good (and hence failing to perform the morally right[6] action) one makes the (morally) evil choice of preferring the good aspect[7] of some morally evil course of behaviour to the good which one ought to choose. Thus if envious one prefers the security given by the contemplation of another's lesser fortune to a shared joy in his good fortune. Anyhow, though a perfectly good will be not the rule yet the judgment "X is good" is not in its own nature affected where the commitment of approval is absent. We do not always approve what we may know to be worthy of approval, i.e. good.

We cannot now shrink from seeking a further specification of goodness, upon the reality of which, as final ground for approval, we have insisted. Of course one may say that we have only made this necessary reality a part of the *nominal* essence of goodness, as being inseparable, that is, from our language,

---

[6] It is characteristic of the moral aspect of life that concerned entities, such as actions, can be rendered totally evil morally through a lack of just one due property. Ontologically, however, nothing positively real is evil. This is why the claim that fornication is or can be great fun is not a compelling moral argument in its favour. In morals one is judging an action as perfecting a man or a woman as a whole, with a view, that is, to the unifying ultimate end of their nature (identifiable in one way or another as a participation in a common good) and, hence, of their existence. This, it will be argued here, is the ultimate *rationale* of obligation, which in this sense alone is thus irreducibly hypothetical, remaining absolute only in the sense of being unchanging as referred to any number of actions of the same identifiable type.

[7] This will of course correspond to some *end*, in itself, like all ends, good.

but it only confuses the issue to start calling this overly modest achievement "internal realism" (if only because it belongs already to the nominal essence of realism that it be "external"). As complement to this, however, we claimed that moral *discourse* itself referred us directly and necessarily to a real or practical world of actions and their moral qualities which is independent (because it *is* independently) of that discourse.

Thus the axiom that one ought to do good and avoid evil differs from saying that one ought to do what one thinks is good and avoid what one thinks is evil, however true this thought may be. For we at times think (or have thought) something good which is or was not good and in this case the pursual of such an end fell under our duty by the second axiom but not by the first. Only if the action of doing what one thinks is good (when it is bad) were itself, in addition, judged good could this then be brought under the first axiom, but by a further judgment or axiom not included in it. Hence they are different. The first axiom requires, in a way that the second does not, that we *critically* appraise our own thoughts, intuitions, beliefs and associated inner impressions in moral matters. So it is certainly not equivalent to the empty assertion that one ought to do what one ought to do. It entails rather that certain actions, should they be good (i.e. should they pursue good ends without intentionally damaging other goods), ought *therefore* to be done. This leaves open a possibility of there being other, non-good actions which ought to be done, unless we go on to equate, as we generally do, the non-good with the evil actions which the principle tells us to avoid. *Actus humanus* as defined by Aquinas, for example, leaves no room for a third class of indifferent acts. It is to be feared that the marginalization of ethics in the public sphere, or in *realpolitik*, complained of in our first chapter, results in great part from a notion that there can be such morally indifferent acts.

In any case, though, "That which is good" stands to "What ought to be done?" as "That which nourishes" stands to "What ought to be eaten?". It does not stand to it as "That which is edible" stands to the latter question. Doing what one ought, all the same, is itself good (as an exercise of the virtue of justice) and so it does in fact follow from the principle that one ought to do what one ought, though one could never make the converse derivation.

What we have emphasised is the cause and effect relation, i.e. precisely that vital relation which a discussion bounded by consideration of "truth conditions" must ignore. X ought to be done *because* X is good, but X is not good because X ought to be done, even though the truth of a statement that X ought to be done would be sufficient reason for X's goodness. Thus we say "They are at home because they expect a visitor" in a recognizably different sense of "because" from where we might say "They are at home because the lights are on", really meaning "I know that they are at home because the lights are on". "Because", as referring to a cause more than a reason, will always be clumsy here, and so we more justly, and hence elegantly, say "The lights are on, so they are at home" or "*Since* the lights are on they must be at home", the necessity introduced by "must" being one of truth rather than of being or nature.

Scepticism about the cause and effect relation is not admissible here because the idea of morality is itself directed to the practical or real sphere. To have consented to philosophize within ethics is already to have rejected scepticism, a view of course implying that the various formalist post-Kantian (and Kantian) systems are unviable, i.e. unliveable. Moreover the causality invoked is not just contingent. In all worlds one ought to do the good, and that not because "good" has been so defined but because its goodness obliges us. Similarly ice chills, not because ice is so defined but because it has that effect. Thus the question remains: what is this goodness?[8]

What is good, we may safely say, is what has value and is hence worthy of desire. Better, it is what has worth and is hence desirable. In this sense, if one must consider what one desires as being of worth, good is what all desire. There is no call to exclude the moral good from this general analysis; that would anyhow make the moral good only equivocally good, as those who despise it generally believe.[9] Regarding morality, however, we have to ask what sort of actions (i.e. as specified by what sort of *ends*) have worth such that they are desirable and thus good, so that they ought to be performed (these ends ought to be pursued) or at least aimed at, whether as means or as ends. It might seem that we can only answer this in terms of other goods already acknowledged. Beyond that, therefore, any search for further justification of the natural moral stance would be nonsensical, which is why Aristotle declared ethics to be unintelligible to the badly brought up. This does not, however, exclude a metaphysical *explanation* of the significance of goodness and hence of the term "good", in terms of being as presented to the will, perhaps. This is the Thomist explanation, according to which goodness, like truth, is an *ens rationis*, and the only actual reality is being, without any autonomous world of "values" lying alongside it, still less of truths (the "third realm" of Frege).

Such explanation, however, is of a term presupposed as understood before ethics or, indeed, any consideration of praxis whatever even begins. There goods are justified as goods only in terms of more basic, so to say given goods

---

[8] See our *Philosophy or Dialectic?*, introductory chapter, for an illustration as to how "dialectical" habits of thought can obscure this question even against one's best intentions.

[9] At first sight Maritain, *op. cit.* p.21, might seem to disagree. He writes

> The idea of the good which I have when I eat a well-ripened fruit and say "That's good," is not the same as when I say "To forgive is good and beautiful."

But he adds, speaking of value, that "It is because it is a valid and legitimate idea in metaphysics that we can understand that it is legitimate and necessary in morality"(p.22).

and so a search for objective principles of value must in some sense be an investigation of existing or customary moral positions. There is just no *source* for any new moral judgment and hence it is conspicuous that the revolutionary teachings of Jesus, say, are squarely founded upon existing values, love of enemies, for example, upon love of neighbour ("Who is my neighbour?" is the question eliciting the injunction to love enemies, i.e. as neighbours), forgiveness upon the customary praise of the divine forgivingness, making us like God, and so on. This refers us back, again, to Foot's remarks. The "background" means that morality cannot be (morally) questioned from outside, only from inside, and hence that it can never be totally eradicated.

There are of course customary principles which mutually conflict, while it might also seem to be a difficulty that this doctrine inherently limits the scope of freedom of conscience. But the difficulty is illusory. Conscience is naturally built up through acquaintance with the moral maxims of the community, present and past, here or elsewhere, and the voice of conscience is an awareness of what its bearer has learned, even granted certain definite potentialities, i.e. granted that stable human nature which issues in a relative constancy of human customs and legislation. The autonomy of conscience is nothing other than the necessity lying upon each of us to interpret just this handed down, i.e. traditional, material for ourselves, since we are, by natural necessity, the authors of our own acts.

Where we find conflicts in our source we need only recall that this source, like the aggregate of all human beings who have given it expression, has an organic character. There is, in other words, a body of moral tradition which may be treated as a unity, analogous to the human race despite its internecine wars. It is in fact a unity. But treating a body of material as a unity, as scientists do with the total collection of natural phenomena, means looking for underlying determining principles, by which at least some contradictions will be found to be in appearance alone, while some more eccentric customs will be shown to result from faulty or biased reasoning and may hence be discounted.

All remaining values, goods, principles of good behaviour, will be found to be a fruit of just one principle or of just one consistent set of principles. In a sense there will have to be just one fundamental principle if of any two principles there is some quality in virtue of which they are both moral or, rather, let us say it, good. Justice, in a similar way, is said to be the form of all the virtues and the term "legal justice", in Thomism, refers to the whole body of possible virtuous actions regarded under the aspect of duty, of what is owed. In Christian doctrine this formal role is played by the higher or ultimate *iustitia* or "righteousness" which is charity.

But if, all the same, we did come down to two or more irreconcilables then we could wonder whether the other valuations were all or some derived jointly from these, or whether any particular valuation derived from just one or other of them but not both (if we suppose two). Now if the ultimates have nothing in common with one another (as they cannot, since that common element would then itself become a single ultimate) then the latter alternative would seem to have to be the case. For they then appear to be contradictory (and not, by the way, just contrary). But then no rational moral judgment can incorporate them both.

In such a case, therefore, we would be forced to choose between the two sets of principles for our source of value. But we identified value with what is good and hence it is that of two contradictory principles if one is good the other is bad and therefore not a source of value. This would mean, does mean, that some value judgments have been made which do not have value and are therefore no justifying source of further valuations.

One recommendation for distinguishing the good from the bad has been that we should follow the opinions of the best or wisest men (*sapientes*). But of course we only consider them the best men where we already share their opinions and approve the actions which they dictate, although manifestation of *prophetic* power, wonder-working and so on, may be considered as a way of breaking out of this circle, i.e. it may be considered in philosophy or theology.

What one can say is that the wish to embrace good principles is already in itself to have embraced one good principle if it is good to desire good. Therefore to begin with that wish, if we could, would be to have already escaped the danger of embracing evil, if indeed there are two moral systems in the world. "A man of good will" could only embrace evil principles by mistake, chance or accident. If he retained his good will long enough, therefore, then rational analysis of his principles and of experience would lead him increasingly out of error.

This means that evil moral principles, if they exist, are not just analogous to factual errors. They are chaotic contradictions of themselves. This follows from our identification of what has value and what is good. There can be only one set of values for there is only one value, the good. A Thomist would say that it is ultimate reality as presented to the will, the good life being seen as one lived in the light of truth, of the truth of being. We might just add that the good, these good principles of goodness, cannot be conceived of as having had a beginning, if all valuation rests on previous valuation. So moral laws are not made, like "positive" laws. They are eternal and, as treated here, can be seen to constitute that one eternal law identified by Augustine, for example, with the divine nature in its capacity of governor of the universe.

*

* *

We mentioned justice as a unifying reality in moral theory. Thus, just as C. Stevenson, working in a positivist milieu, in his *Ethics and Language*[10] attempted to isolate from the confused sea of twentieth century moral language the notion of *approval* and to set up a kind of canonization of it as what he called a "working model", so we, with better reason, might set up the notion of obligation as a working model, as a concept, indeed, of central ethical importance, since without it there is no ethics. Even utilitarians set forth their principle as being the one which one *ought* to follow, as one ought, they are quite sure, to follow reason.

It is fair to say that people are concerned over the possibility that they have done those things which they ought not to have done, or that they have left undone those things which they ought to have done. They are concerned, that is, about their moral obligations, in a different way to how they might be concerned about other people's approval. This was introduced with a special emphasis into human culture under the idea of pleasing God rather than men, which finds its philosophical counterpart in the absolutization of obligation, God being definitionally the source of all things and of all concepts. Justice, for example, is henceforth seen to mean that we are absolutely obliged to honour even our obligations to contingent created beings. In this perspective Kant committed the error of absolutizing the *concept* of absoluteness itself (as a clear and distinct idea), cutting it loose even from the absolute being.

Even if people could be deluded in thinking that moral obligation exists, yet this would witness to its existence as a concept, which might well be made a "working model". People always want to know whether what is recommended coincides with what they in fact ought to do. Obligations, that is, are conceived of as real if invisible, while prescriptive or emotive theories simply offer a different concept for our consideration. In no sense do they offer a reductive analysis of the original concept of moral obligation. One might more fruitfully explore the idea of an *analogy* between obligation and prescription, though this would not of itself imply that that the latter were an important ethical topic.

Obligation as a notion entails that something is *owed*, owed as money, but also gratitude, is owed. In morals it is actions that are owed and so in some sense the term brings morals under a wider department of human life, that of transactions generally. But by the same token it is reductive of moral reality since morals as anciently understood should be the widest department of all, coinciding with the project of a man's whole life, and hence it is that moral theory, in the doctrine of the cardinal virtues, extends beyond considerations of justice and obligation, even though a precept can be said to correspond to each virtue. The doctrine of the unity of the virtues means that you can't have

[10] Newhaven 1944.

one virtue without the others, as the truly just man has to be loving and merciful. Allowing for this interplay of the virtues makes the task of those who want to analyse clear and distinct ideas more difficult, but it is ignored at the price of misrepresentation of human reality.

The question "Why should I do my duty?" is as empty as the question "Why should I pay my debts?" A debt is only a debt because it is what I should pay. As such, it is already an example of an owed action. The whole monetary system depends upon a moral concept.

*

* *

In a deeper sense, we have suggested, obligation corresponds to the requirement to be, or to become, what one is, to "grow up" one might almost say, this being an essential condition for happiness, i.e. for the flourishing of our specific nature. The question is: do we make a reduction in analysing obligation in this way? We might ask if we are obliged to prefer being to nothingness, but it should make us suspicious that nothingness is an abstraction. If we rephrase the question in terms of preferring being to nothing it becomes at once ambiguous, since there is no nothing to which being can be preferred. One is not free to prefer being, since being is what is essentially desirable, i.e. good, though good, a name for being as falling under the will, is an *ens rationis*. It is really no different from being. Suicide only seems a counter-example, since there is always something, i.e. a being, perhaps a liberation, which the suicide seeks. It seems then that to see obligation as the condition for fulfilment is not to make it reductively hypothetical, any more than to see evil as essentially posterior to good is to make evil less thoroughly evil than it can be. Those who spurn the moral law unmake themselves. No weightier sanction is conceivable. Even the evil of disobedience to God is to be explained in this way, since God, as God, the ground of our own being. There is no other kind of God to talk about.

The point at issue is rather the less profound one, viz. whether to assert the reality of moral obligation *is* to acknowledge God. Any other *basis* for obligation does seem to make it hypothetical, even though it is nonsense to say it can have no basis. For example, moral duty is for ordinary purposes explicable in terms of the common good, something other and distinct from the aggregate good of the utilitarians. Those actions are absolutely prohibited which harm the common good of humanity, as does killing the innocent or adultery, it is generally considered. But the sinner can contemn the common good; it is his choice. As such it does not yet contain the notion of an absolute and final failure, which to be such would have to be eternally experienced. Absolute obligation thus appears correlate with eternal punishment, the ultimate sanction. In divorcing it from all sanction Kant dissolved the very notion of an absoluteness in reality. The reason to which he referred was no longer practical, but speculative, and obligation is only retained as a pure concept, like a number. The Kantian ethic is incapable of application. I cannot act as if I could will something as a universal law unless I am convinced that there are universal laws.

Chapter 6

Hypothetical Morality and Institutional Double-Truth

We will pursue these matters further. It is true that in the field of human action almost all that we do or can be obliged to do is elected or laid upon us for the sake of some further end. But if we were to view morality as essentially a hypothetical matter this would mean that we were cutting off those ends themselves from the sphere of the moral or of moral precepts.[1] The choice of aims, plans of life and so on is then left entirely open.

Because of the demonstrable nature of human action as including purpose within itself such an openness must inevitably react back upon our choice of means, i.e. of actions. Absurdly, we can be led to saying that we choose our obligations, that morality is made up of "elective principles"[2]. But in this case, although inevitably issuing linguistically into the categorical "should", morality is bogus. One should rather say that along this road one cannot account for morality; not all ends can be treated as optional.

The approach is in fact a mere reaction to moralism. Along with the attitude against which it is reacting this approach fails to consider that human purposes, the ends to which actions are means, might themselves be included in morality's purview as the whole reason why the moral dimension is found in discourse at all. As Aquinas puts it,

> Even if the goodness of an action is not caused by the goodness of its effect, yet an action is called good from this, that it is able to bring in (*inducere*) a good effect; and thus the very proportion of an action to its (sc. intended) effect is the index (*ratio*) and essence of its own goodness.[3]

On its own the main force of this text can seem to lie in its massive common sense. This however merely reinforces a quality of discrimination and thorough analysis which as practised throughout this question of the *Summa*, "On the Goodness and Badness of Human Actions", give

---

[1] Many authors follow this road, e.g. P. Foot, "Morality and Art", *Proceedings of the British Academy* 56 (1970); John Kekes, "Happiness", *Mind*, July 1982. J. Finnis, in *Natural Law and Natural Rights* (Oxford 1980), argues, following Rawls and of course Hare, for the optional character of ends chosen (cf. section V.6 and page 132). Even Peter Geach, in *The Virtues* (Cambridge 1976), moves in the same direction when he speaks of faith as a virtue needed for the success of any enterprise whatever.

[2] Foot, *op. cit.*

[3] I.e. it is what we *mean* by its goodness. Aquinas, *Summa theol.* Ia-IIae 18, 2 ad 3um.

the strongest grounds for accepting its conclusions, including the one cited.

Not considering human purposes morally, making *unexamined* happiness a raw prerequisite of moral theory, is actually as Kantian as the type of deontologism which this attitude opposes. For along with Kant it fails to make sense of the indispensable notion of obligation, i.e. it does not address the idea of an ethics. Instead it merely takes over the notion of obligation with which Kant left us in order to reject obligation as such. Now Kant, in excluding all consideration of happiness or of ends as a principle of moral evaluation, rendered obligation unintelligible, but retained it since "respect for the law", he rightly saw, cannot consistently be abandoned.

The advocates of "hypothetical morality", unlike Kant, see that there cannot be obligation divorced from purpose, but they equate this with the different position that there are no moral laws which bind unless we want them to bind, which actually returns us to Kant's voluntarism, the law one respects being nothing other than one's own will, to which Kant ascribes the requisite dignity precisely because, as he claimed, it is bound to no end. There is a certain circularity.

The way out of this, if we should be in it, is to acknowledge that moral obligation attaches primarily to the *ends* of human action, since these specify acts in their kind. The necessity of these ends[4] is not of course a necessity of compulsion (*coactio*), but of the bond of justice.[5] This necessity of duty, the obligation of precept, is only to be explained through the necessity of some purpose (i.e. of some end purposed), necessary indeed in the strictly moral sense that the end of virtue itself cannot be attained without it. One's primary or *per se* duty is not the mere phenomenal motions of the action, but "that which is the end, because this is what has the essential intelligibility of some good," i.e. of something that we value and hence aim at. Hence the action itself, as ordered to the end, is only owed or a duty *propter aliud*.[6] Laws or precepts are for the sake of purposes or ends, and it is those actions which have as essential to their purpose objects which are incompatible with our human fulfilment (end) which are categorically forbidden.

So it is quite wrong to restrict the sphere of obligation and law to the actions by which we attain our ends, as if we were to say to soldiers that it did not matter morally whether they aimed to kill the enemy or their own men; the main thing was to shoot straight and clean.

Given then that we have at least negative reason to look for the root of moral obligation in certain basic purposes, common to all if obligations are common to

---

[4] Cf. Aristotle, *Nic. Eth.* III, 113b.

[5] *Ex obligatione*. Cf. Aquinas, *Summa theol.* IIa-IIae 58, 3 ad 2um. I know of no later account which puts things as perspicuously.

[6] *Ibid.* 44, 1.

all, what will indicate these purposes to us, and in virtue of what do they get their obligatory force? These are actually the two important, often neglected questions about ethics. It would seem obvious that our purposes are conditioned to the extent that our human nature is conditioned, and even though rational nature such as ours is in a real sense open or *ad opposita*, the condition for free judgment, yet such a nature derives all its dignity through being orientated towards the good as such, *bonum in communi*, by no means a notion without content but corresponding to our most basic inclination, in terms of which the specific inclinations of each of our natural faculties is to be understood. The question as to what might give these inclinations (to our natural ends), or anything else, obligatory force we have discussed in earlier chapters. The answer means that we cannot settle for the system of hypothetical imperatives, having made our corrective insertion of purposes into the moral scheme. We cannot just airily mention that we are "apt to be haunted by the thought of a law-giver."[7] There is only a haunting if there is a ghost, i.e. a spirit.

We should notice here what, harking back to thirteenth century controversies at the University of Paris, one might well call institutionalized Averroism. It was followers of Averroes in the arts faculty at Paris who played the main part in separating the teaching of philosophy from that of theology, at least in so far as the latter had revelation for its object. The tendency is sharpened when, under the influence of the political laicism of the modern era, philosophy becomes regarded as a "secular subject". One ought to remember that it was not thus secular for the pre-Christian founders of philosophy. Plato frequently has recourse to divine tradition, while for Aristotle, metaphysics was both "first philosophy" and theology.

So in reading Foot or Anscombe, for example, one encounters a developed professional attitude obedient to this influence, but which obscures fair representation of the issues involved. The axiom that theology ought not to make a difference is accepted without examination, and not enough care is taken to distinguish theistic philosophy from Christian theology. Thus Foot quite clearly feels that basing obligation upon a divine law-giver is enough to put it out of court without discussion, while Anscombe, having argued that this is in fact the basis, goes on to suggest that modern philosophy accordingly give up consideration of it.[8] Alan Donagan, while rejecting Anscombe's view, lauds Kant as one who "arrived at the position that the common morality he learned from his pietist parents was after all not a matter of revelation or of feeling, but of ordinary human reason,"[9] as if this were not also the Stoic and Scholastic

---

[7] Foot, *op. cit.* p. 17.

[8] G.E.M. Anscombe, "Modern Moral Philosophy", *Philosophy* 1958. It is possible that the suggestion is made ironically.

[9] Donagan, *op. cit.* p.148.

position. They, however, contrary to Kant, were quite explicit that "ordinary human reason" derived its legislative power from its divine origin (also a key Augustinian position) and must ground its justification of that power in explicit acknowledgement of this origin.[10]

What is rejected here, as if confused with dogmatic theology, is natural or philosophical theology as part, the crowning part, of philosophy. This move is of course contrary to pre-Socratic and all classical tradition, continued and at its most explicit in Descartes and Leibniz, whatever the shortcomings of their defence of it.

But if, anyhow, Anscombe is right then, contrary to her suggestion, moral philosophy *must* concern itself with God. The project of replacing the language of obligation with something benignly elective is merely absurd, psychologically in the first place. Choosing, for example, to defend the rights of the unborn has no meaning unless I think that they have those rights and that I have the corresponding obligations. Nor should anyone be prejudiced in advance by the consideration that an argument for the existence of God can be derived from the fact, if it be a fact, of obligation. Let us rather discuss the argument together with its premisses. This might be *the* fundamental question of ethics.

---

[10] This, of course, is also the basis upon which Sartre and his school reject moral obligation.

Chapter 7

Kant and the Uniquely Good Will

> Nothing can possibly be conceived in the world, or even out of it, which can be called good without qualification, except a good will.

This statement, from Kant's *Groundwork of the Metaphysics of Morals*[1], has in the two succeeding centuries often been put forward as a self-evident principle, which it is even a mark of rectitude to be able to intuit. Yet it seems plainly false. We stand as it were at the source of those approaches which we have so deprecated in previous chapters, even though Kant too has his ancestors.

Kant's arguments in support of the principle include the consideration that "other gifts of nature may also become extremely bad... if the will... is not good," a consideration which applies equally, he thinks, to "gifts of fortune", happiness and the virtues themselves. These are "far from deserving to be called good without qualification, although they have been so unconditionally praised by the ancients," for, after all, such virtues of "moderation in the affections and passions, self-control and calm deliberation" can be of help in performing bad acts, acts, one supposes, conceived in despite of the categorical imperative.

*

*   *

Kant has failed to notice here, it would seem, that also a good will can be of help to *another* person of evil will who uses good people for evil ends. A state headed by a ruler planning an evil war is made "far more dangerous" if populated by dutiful tax-payers and so on and even "more abominable". Thus utilitarians use the same argument as Kant, though in this interpersonal sense, to discredit conscientiousness. It is however the same argument, for the fact that I cannot exploit my own good will as I can my moderation and the other virtues is a truth about the human constitution, not a mysteriously special kind of goodness in the good will.

Thus, on the contrary, it seems that happiness and the gifts of nature other than the virtues can remain good without qualification even if subject to abuse, i.e. by others, and this precisely because they are not moral goods, i.e. goods proper to human action. As for abuse by the person possessing them, of which

[1] Abbott's translation, New York 1949. All Kant quotations in English are from this text.

Kant speaks, it is precisely because they remain thus good that we say that they are abused, except in the case of the virtues. These moral goods, by contrast, simply cannot be abused. Thus, on an Aristotelian view, the fearlessness of a murderer *in actu* can never be courage, since courage is a species of right ordering of the soul.[2] The doctrine of the unity of the virtues is pertinent here. Courage is just as much "good without qualification" as is a good will, i.e. it is just as much a moral good. All ontological goods too, however, are also good without qualification, unless the qualification be referred to the finite limitation of their being, in which case it applies equally to any created, finite good will.

Reference to the right ordering of the soul might seem to reintroduce the uniquely good will, but this is to forget that the ordering is made right, in the nature of things, by what the soul is ordered towards, so that if this *end* be not "good without qualification" then it will be arbitrary to say that the will to it is good.

In fact it is just the Kantian good will which is most easily exploitable as a mere moralistic posture, since he has deliberately isolated it from prudence and the other virtues whereas, in the tradition, to have one virtue you must have them all. Since a good will as existing by itself would be weak and easily exploitable it seems better to agree that prudence is as necessary for moral virtue as moral virtue is for prudence.[3]

The fact that no *man*, no human being, is good without a good will does not justify Kant's claim. We need to be clear that the proper subject of moral goodness is a man or woman, not a will. Thus Kant must agree that a man who possesses a good will is also "good without qualification". He might of course reply that it is just such possession which is the qualification, but then, equally, a will has to be thus possessed in order to be good in the first place. Will, that is, is a power of the soul and not a substantial thing at all, not a primary being such as might be good on its own or without qualification.

The background to this improper way of speaking, with its false consequences, was prepared earlier than Kant's time. Thus Duns Scotus often speaks of the will (rather than the man) as itself an agent. *Voluntas vult*, the will wills; it is the *indeterminatum* which *potest se determinare*, the indeterminate (thing) which can determine itself.[4] Aquinas, by contrast, is mostly careful to refer to the "will, according to which *someone* naturally wills."[5]

A good will, all agree, is a necessary condition for there being a good man. Now by a good man we naturally understand a morally good man. But this of

---

[2] Cf. J. Smith, "Can Virtue Be in the Service of Bad Acts: a Response to Philippa Foot", *The New Scholasticism* 1984.

[3] Cf. Aquinas, *Summa theol.* Ia-IIae 58, 4 & 5.

[4] J. Duns Scotus, *Expositio in XII libros Metaphysicorum Aristotelis, XV.*

[5] Aquinas, *Ibid.* Ia, 82, 1 ad 2um.

itself gives no occasion to distinguish moral goodness as a different type of goodness from the others, otherwise we might do the same for architectural goodness just because by a good building we naturally understand an architecturally good building. Moral goodness is simply the goodness of human actions, such actions following immediately upon the dynamic human essence (*operatio sequitur esse*); since man, as rational, has free choice of will, moral goodness is related to use of freedom. Far from being a different, equivocal kind of goodness it gives the conditions under which a free being can become or remain good *simpliciter*. As a faculty the will is good or bad as is any other. That for moral goodness it is uniquely essential to have a good will does not make such a will uniquely good. For the reason for this unique essentialness is not a moral reason at all, but simply the fact that "will determines the use to which everything else in us is put."[6]

Thus the non-moral, natural goodness of the will as a power of the soul determines, when it follows reason, the *moral* goodness of the man. So "beings with wills are called good when those wills are good." But the good will is the condition for the goodness only of "beings with wills", not of everything "in the world or even out of it." Hence "a man is called bad when he fails to be virtuous, and an eye bad when its vision fails."[7] There is not a difference of *sense*. That virtue is needed, again, depends on the fact of human freedom, that the powers of the soul, unlike those (its virtues) of the eye, are not of themselves *determinatae ad unum* without the "right ordering" mentioned, for which we are responsible.

It might seem that Kant could claim support from the classical division of goodness (*bonum*) into *honestum*, *utile* and *delectabile*. Yet here it is not only the *bonum honestum* which is good without qualification. Of its kind a glass of beer is equally good (indeed, beer which had the freedom to jump out of its glass at the wrong moment would be, as beer, rather bad). Aquinas comments: *haec divisio non est per oppositas res, sed per oppositas rationes*,[8] i.e. the goodness of disparate things is not itself varied, as if only some or one of them were *truly* good, but only the ways in which (the same) goodness can be attributed to various things (like a function, as Geach suggested). Goodness and badness as such are found in a whole range of things of which human wills are just one instance. The whole apparatus of descriptivity *vis à vis* prescriptivity only comes in *epistemologically* because of the freedom of wills. It has nothing to do ontologically with the goodness involved, but with our way of getting to it. Of course the moral instance is of special interest to us, who are responsible for the quality of our own being as we are not for that of those

---

[6] *Ibid.* Ia 5, 4 ad 3um.
[7] *Ibid.* Ia 5, 3 ad 2um.
[8] *Ibid.* 5, 6 ad 2um.

we observe outside of us, but it is the non-ambiguity of "good" which gives point to the required moral strife, which would otherwise be a futile exercise in priggishness, i.e. if moral goodness were only equivocally good.

These seem to me decisive reasons for rejecting Kant's master-idea and, hence, the popular version of autonomy which derives from it. Kant, however, pushes his idea to the limit. A will is good "not because of what it performs or effects... but simply by virtue of the volition... the summoning of all means in our power." Volition here seems to correspond to intention, and Kant is surely not indifferent to *what* is intended. He wishes though to reduce this in the first place, for the good will, to the fulfilment of duty as such. But to intend fulfilment of duty is to intend to intend whatever should be intended. We may take it, however, that *all* intention, to be such, includes intention of fulfilment of the intention.

But now such an intention is as much a definite "what" as any other object of will. It is not "second order" in any formally interesting sense. One sets one's will on this one thing. Even the will just to do what is right could only be justified if this were judged a *good* intention, like an intention to give alms. There is nothing that is more *formal* about it. For Kant too, therefore, the will's goodness depends on the *use* to which one intends to put "everything else in us". For this intention (of fulfilling duty), like any other, remains in force even though he bids us prescind from its effectiveness. All the same, his principle that he who wills the end will also the means presumably comes into effect here, "ought" implying "can" in the sense which he explains.

Thus if the will is "not, to be sure, a mere wish, but the summoning of all means in our power" then it seems that the good will can never "wholly lack power to accomplish its purpose". For to *try* to do something is always itself to do something (else)[9], even if only to summon. Willing, that is, is prior in nature to performance but not in time (St. Anselm); it is intentional or "other-directed", and its goodness *must* be judged in terms of what it is directed to. But then we cannot say that everything else is good by virtue of it alone, even as there is no concept of duty separable from conceptions of the moral law, such, for instance, as those of justice which the very notion of duty (*debitum*) presupposes. It is because lying is bad without qualification that the will not to lie, or do anything else bad, is good without qualification.

So the resolve to obey the moral precepts obeys a precept of the same kind as the others, the law that law is to be obeyed being no different in form from the law that murder is not to be committed. Such obedience, however, as everyone knows, is just what Kant's system would exclude. His stress on duty corresponds rather to a right relation to the rational (though one would think that the motivation for achieving this must also fall under duty). But

[9] Cf. G.E.M. Anscombe & P.T. Geach, *Three Philosophers*, Oxford 1967, p.108.

this, we will see, rests upon a mistaken theory of practical reasoning. We only reach a meta-level when we ask, if we do, *what* gives reason its right or authority.

*

*   *

Kant's idea of pure duty, pure will, in fact needs to be buttressed with a materialistic conception of happiness:

> For all the actions which a creature has to perform with a view to this purpose (sc. happiness) and the whole rule of its conduct, would be far more surely prescribed to it by instinct, and the end would have been attained thereby much more certainly than it ever can be by reason.

He adds that

> our existence has a different and far nobler end, for which, and not for happiness, reason is properly intended.

One wonders how the attainment of *this* end can do other than *ipso facto* contribute to happiness, unless it is not an end of *ours*. In fact Kant will say that it is not, the end being the rational creature, indifferently I or another, who is an end in himself.

This schema could not have been so easily drawn up if Kant had acknowledged the more normal human ideal of happiness to which the rational activities of knowledge and love are essential, instead of opposing happiness to the rational. There is a not often marked convergence here with utilitarianism, separating both systems profoundly from traditional teleological ethics. This is why to consider traditional teleological ethics and utilitarianism together as "consequentialist" so confuses the issue. The real divide is between those who divorce the *motive* of happiness from the moral motive and those who do not do so.

The utilitarians in fact react against Kant on Kant's own terms. But the middle position is that the virtues and the precepts that serve them are in themselves the directions to the goal, i.e. to happiness, in which they to some extent participate. *De ratione praecepti est quod importet ordinem ad finem*, i.e. it belongs to the very idea of a duty (*ratio debiti*) that it be imposed for some purpose (*ex necessitate alicuius finis*).[10]

*

*   *

[10] Aquinas, *Summa theol.* Ia-IIae 99, 1.

The theory of ends in themselves which are higher than happiness, viz. human beings, to whom reason demands that an altruistic regard be paid, depends upon Kant's idiosyncratic account of practical reason according to which reason can be practical "in its own right" or without becoming a "slave of the passions". Kant expends much effort outlining an apparently purely negative version of a practical reason which is not an instrument of wants. "What the conclusion of such reasoning prescribes is not anything wanted or desired at all," as Alan Donagan approvingly sums it up.[11] The two related gains which Kant wishes to draw from this account is a theory of practical reason as able to choose its own ends, by means of an elected "plan of life" in the modern jargon, and, secondly, a theory of ends in themselves, i.e. non-producible, because actually existent ends.

It is essential to this project to show that there are two kinds of human willing possible, viz. rational and non-rational:

> Whoever wills an end, inasmuch as he wills rationally, wills also the indispensably necessary means to it, if they are in his power.

This is claimed to be "analytic", and indeed it is true that in general we do not will the end just in so far as we do not will the means. Otherwise we are concerned with velleities rather than with willing. One would like a certain gratification, but prefers to preserve one's honour; but if one *wills* it, why then one casts honour aside, if that is the necessary means.

So if this is the force of "rational" then it seems that *all* willing is rational and that we have here a (speculative) account of what wanting or willing is. But then the account cannot be made out simultaneously as a practical "hypothetical" imperative to will the means if one wills the end, as if it were possible to will in some other way, or to post a letter without putting it into the box. The suggestion, in the formulation of the "ground of imperatives of skill", that human willing can ever be other than rational in this sense leads to the mistaking of a speculative description of willing for a practical prescription that one make a choice, not of this or that, but as such.

This abstract pseudo-requirement is then substituted for the Aristotelian *bonum est persequendum*, where *bonum* refers to man's natural ultimate end, i.e. his happiness, as the controlling and constitutive directive of practical reason. But one cannot prescribe as a practical or moral consequence of a situation (that of wanting something) an action that is logically necessary for that situation to obtain (viz. wanting the means to it).

We already noted this *petitio principii* in noting that wanting to do something was a matter of summoning the means in our power, doing something else. We noted that willing was prior in nature but not in time to performance,

[11] *Op. cit.* p. 214.

i.e. to some performance or other. One wills the means *in* the end or else one does not will *that* end. The "analytic" statement does not direct anything.

Weakness of will is not the proof by example that Kant would require, as if it consisted in refusing to make this proto-choice or decision to exercise freedom by making choices. More typically it merely shows a failure to want a certain goal as much as one pretends, because there is some other end that one wants more, such as ease, pleasure, wealth. One always wants something, it being our nature to tend to the apprehended good. This in fact is what makes a want a want, and not some voluntaristic choice, ancestor of the "plan of life" theories.

Of course if one's dignity consisted in making choices in a void then something would have to set limits to this. Here reason imposes an "unconditional rational end... without presupposing any particular moral position,"[12] such as that of Aristotle. It is all at a meta-level. "Rational nature exists as an end in itself."

Arguing for this as a foundation for altruism via the entirely negative claim that in deliberation we are not "subject to" our desires does not go through, however. This would be not so much free will as wilfulness, to which no special dignity attaches. He who deliberates over means is free, indeed, just because he deliberates. But this should not imply a freedom *from desire* as such. This would be a pointless freedom rather than one conferring a dignity, as Sartre saw when, starting from similar premisses, he likened it to a hole in being. One cannot patch up this hole with ends-in-themselves which are accorded their value solely by themselves being such holes in the first place.

> ...by the very fact that it supersedes all the producible ends set up by instinct and desire, reason provides man with an end of quite another sort,

writes Donagan. But if reason is not determined by any ends at all then one cannot see in virtue of what it can be rational in any positive sense to relinquish (or adopt) a given particular end. One cannot appeal to the ends-in-themselves since they are only to be established as conclusion of the argument.

This at best benign circularity is Kant's greatest strength. All his concepts hang together in a consistent ideology. It appears all the same, as we noted at the start, that the existential point at which to pierce the circle is his notion of the uniquely good will, clearly derived from a culturo-religious context and clearly, one has tried to show, misconceived. Even after that there would remain the "grammatical" objection, viz. how can a nature, a substance, itself *be* an end or a purpose?

---

[12] *Ibid.* p.226.

Chapter 8

R.M. Hare's Metaethics

We take now a closer look at one of Kant's contemporary imitators (one can hardly say that he has had successors). The group are in general recognizable as taking what we elsewhere call the anti-ontological stance. This, after an initial period of psychologizing, has led ineluctably to a reduction of the science of ethics to what its protagonists rather grandly call metaethics, which amounts to not much more than the analysis of ethical language, "the language of morals".

This phrase, of course, is the title of R.M. Hare's first important book[1]. His work typifies the approach, as the first sentence of his second book[2] shows:

> The function of moral philosophy - at any rate the hope with which I study it — is that of helping us to think better about moral questions by exposing the logical structure of the language in which this thought is expressed.

A fair comment to this would be that if moral philosophy's function is only to help us to think about moral questions, exclusively by analysing language, then its function cannot be to actually think about moral questions, as opposed to just helping us to think about them. Hare does after all say *the* function, not *a* function.

Of course if he had spoken of helping us to make better moral decisions then his statement would be less puzzling, and one does indeed find in him a tendency to conflate decision-making with the passing of moral judgment.[3] So it is not surprising that he leaves little place for the philosophical moralist who, we have noted, does not always practice what he preaches. He is as it were eliminated by the definite article, as ethics is replaced by "value-free" metaethics, nothing else being considered scientific. This negates Aristotle's assertion that the first principles of this science are supplied by the customs of human society. But the heightened rigour, if it is that, means that moral thought proper is left to the ordinary man in the street and clerics, as henceforth a field for guesses, supported by beer, emotion or authority, not by critical reason.

---

[1] R.M. Hare, *The Language of Morals*, Oxford 1952.

[2] *Freedom and Reason*, Oxford 1965.

[3] He conflates the non-verbal with the verbal, according to Philippa Foot. Cf. Theron, *Morals as Founded on Natural Law*, pp.43-45. But Hare says explicitly that "Moral disputes are not purely verbal" (*Freedom and Reason*, p.28). Indeed, but then neither are zoological disputes, which are nonetheless conducted in clear separation from decision-making. Cf. Theron, *Philosophy or Dialectic?* Part II, chapter 1.

Traditional writers on ethics were concerned not just with language and its logic, though this aspect of things by no means escaped them, but with reality. Thus, for example, Gilson:

> Duty is not to be deduced from a revelation, but from a doctrine of creation which is itself deduced from a metaphysic of Being. And this metaphysic of Being is deduced from nothing but the exigencies of rational thought.[4]

To understand the disagreement we would have to go to the roots of Hare's approach, as to some extent we have already done in the case of Kant.

What Hare does is to first set up and then claim to resolve a conflict between freedom and reason. In harmony with this initially confused opposition of two qualities which really belong together like two sides of one coin he will state that although the solution of a moral problem must be rational yet only the person involved can solve it. We have already encountered this differentiation of moral understanding and the virtue of prudence. Hare, however, gives it a rather special twist. He will have it not only that it is the individual who must decide how to act but that he alone "freely" judges how he ought to act. He refers to

> This conviction, which every adult has, that he is free to form his own opinions about moral questions.[5]

Of course he is, we might reply, simply because anyone is free to form opinions about just anything at all. Freedom to form an opinion simply connotes the unconditioned nature of rational judgment as such. This is what constitutes it as rational, since we are not speaking of wanton *assertion* but of the essentially free play of thought.

The ambiguity arises because Hare wants to characterize moral judgments as decisions, without however acknowledging that this is already a rather specific, even a dogmatic move. For prior to establishment of such a view decision and judgment must be allowed to retain their categorically distinct meanings. What Hare does, however, is to blur their distinction from the start by his claim that ethical terms have two types of meaning, the "prescriptive" and the "descriptive". The logical positivist theories of "emotive" meaning had of course made it less startling to introduce this dichotomy of meaning. The novelty of Hare's approach is the systematic assumption that *logic* can and should treat of both types of meaning. It is all part of a very deep-going confusion between the practical and the theoretical. As such it was fundamental already to Wittgenstein's analysis of language.

According to Hare, if someone says "You ought to do X" and he is not using "ought" in an "off-colour way"[6] then, in view of "ought"'s prescriptive

[4] E. Gilson, *The Spirit of Medieval Philosophy*, New York 1940, pp. 362-363.
[5] Hare, *Freedom and Reason*, p.2.
[6] Cf. *Freedom and Reason*, p.83.

meaning, the sentence includes an imperative element, i.e. the action is prescribed and therefore willed. One cannot sincerely say or think that one ought to do something without willing the deed. Sin, conversely, is impossible, as conscience is irresistible. Thus a moral judgment *is* a decision, an act of will.

Hare offers no arguments for this radical view. Instead he argues that non-prescriptivist views are absurd, i.e. views such as that there are objective moral principles known to us and applied in purely "descriptive" moral judgments which are true or false. Of this view Hare writes:

> Such a doctrine would be that of a very hidebound moralist, whose moral principles were a set of copy-book headings.[7]

To back this up he only adds that if moral principles

> (in some sense) exist, I am sure that they do not always exist *antecedently*, so that all we have to do is to consult them,

supporting this with an example from Sartre.

Now of course the other side would agree that one has to do more than "consult" principles like looking up telephone numbers. One should consult them using the virtue of prudence, by which we judge what is to be done by making a true assessment of the "morally relevant features" (Hare's own phrase) of the particular case. Hare himself describes just this process so that one asks what "morally relevant features" could be if they were not either the antecedent principles which bear upon the matter or features made relevant by means of them.

Hare though seems to think that we derive our principles from the situation, not, however, in an inductive way which might correspond to Aristotelian *epagoge*. They are universal only in that we are *prepared* to universalize them to relevantly similar instances. But they are not general. General principles are arrived at later on the basis of experience, mere rules of thumb to save us from practical puzzlement such as a purer situation ethics would give rise to. Thus

> The thesis of universalizability does not require moral judgments to be made on the basis of highly general moral principles of the copy-book-heading type... What the wiser among us do is to think deeply about the crucial moral questions, especially those that face us in our own lives; but when we have arrived at an answer to a particular problem, to crystallize it into a not too specific or detailed form, so that its salient features may stand out and serve us again in a like situation without need for *so much* thought.[8]

One difficulty with this process is that one cannot explain how it ever gets started. How are the first, on the spot judgments made without "antecedent" principles? How are the "morally relevant (salient) features" identified?

---

[7] *Ibid.* p.37.
[8] *Ibid.* p.41.

In general the oddity of Hare's views are chiefly due to his theory of meaning, due in the logical order, that is to say. The psychological *causes* of his preferring such views are no doubt quite other. His theory of meaning, anyhow, stresses that the meaning of descriptive terms and hence of descriptive judgments is "subject to change".[9] Now in virtue of their descriptive element moral judgments too are "universalizable", just as is a purely descriptive judgment such as "This is red". For

> To say that something is red is to say that it is of a certain kind, and so to imply that anything which is of that same kind is red.

The force of this interpretation is not altogether clear, especially when Hare goes on to claim, even to stress, that disputes about such descriptive meaning are "purely verbal"[10]. This is in contrast to moral differences over terms used, which in fact involve "substantial questions of morality". So Hare coins the word *doog to carry the descriptive meaning of "good" without its prescriptive meaning. Anyone saying "X is a *doog man"

> will be committed to the view that some man who was exactly like X, or like him in the relevant respects, would also be a doog man; and the relevant respects would be simply those which the descriptive meaning-rule for the word "doog" specified.

By contrast, if we add "prescriptive meaning" to *doog (which thus becomes "good") then "the descriptive meaning-rule becomes more than a mere meaning-rule."

> In saying that it is proper to call a certain kind of man good... we are not just explaining the meaning of a word; it is not mere verbal instruction we are giving but... *moral* instruction... Our descriptive meaning-rule has thus turned into a synthetic moral principle.[11]

What Hare misses in all this is that in saying that it is proper to call X *doog we *may* be concerned not with meaning-rules but with ascribing the real quality of *doogness to X. Just as if the judge had said "It is proper to call Smerdyakov but not Dmitri Karamazov a murderer (murderous)" he would not have been concerned with the meaning of that term but with the "substantial question" of who was murderous. No blether about "the linguistic idiom of our time"[12] can alter that. The judgment, besides being correct, would be as synthetic as any moral principle, not because of any "prescriptive" element in "murderous" but because it was a factual description of Smerdyakov.

In short, we are not always talking *about* the words we use to talk about other things. So it is not plausible to say that descriptive judgments are "purely

[9] *Ibid.* p.7.
[10] *Ibid.* p.28.
[11] *Ibid.* p.23.
[12] Peter Geach's phrase.

verbal", as if only moral judgments had "substance", or as if the former were not "synthetic". If we try fitting existential statements in amongst Hare's descriptive judgments then we must conclude that whenever one says "Tigers exist" one is merely claiming a use for the term "tiger" (it is proper to call something "tiger"). But one is more probably claiming that there *are* tigers, a perspective from which the lexicographical consequence, however certain or necessary, appears as of only marginal interest. If one could reduce all speech and its meaning to lexicography[13] then of of course moral terms would need, impossibly, a new *kind* of meaning so as to keep their normative weight.

Hare tries to support his case for descriptive judgments being purely verbal by the example of language about trees and bushes.[14] But the reason why it might seem purely verbal whether we *call* a certain plant a tree or a bush is that *in reality* it is not clear that no trees are bushes. In fact his example confessedly concerns a dispute as to *what to regard as* bushes or trees (where only bushes are to be cut down), so it is preconditioned to be purely terminological. Suppose, on the other hand, that the gardeners had been told to shoot the rabbits but to be careful with the piano, or to give the monkeys peanuts but serve tea to the guests, and try arguing that these are purely verbal matters.

Since, then, Hare appears to think that the descriptive element of a moral judgment such as "One ought to do X" is simply something like "It is proper to call X an action that one ought to do" he cannot see it as giving more than verbal instruction unless prescriptiveness and hence imperativeness is added. But from our examples it seems clear that we can mean that X is *in fact* an action that one ought to do, as Smerdyakov was the murderer, and understand by "ought" some quality of a person's putative action as being, for example, owed like a sum of money. But this would be to make it both purely descriptive and yet in the same respect a principle or moral judgment of substance.

So it is clear that it is the defects or peculiarities of Hare's theory of *descriptive* meaning which requires him to postulate prescriptivism. Thus even in his tree and bush example he offers us in place of descriptive judgment what is really a decision (as to what one will call a bush). So the ground is well prepared for moral "judgments" which are really decisions to prescribe and in one's own case to perform certain actions, so running together again the "verbal" and the non-verbal, the speculative and the practical. If there is no place in his system for the judgment proper then this is because there is no acknowledgement of any category or quasi-category of reality as such, of which indeed any judgment must be predicated, on the old theory that the subject "stands for" (*supponit pro*) some being, in itself or of the mind. Instead we have only

---

[13] As one reduces the doctrine of the supposition of terms to a theory of reference consonant with "internal realism".

[14] *Ibid.* pp.28-29.

the logical relations obtaining within moral and other *discourse* which is somehow just given, a self-contradictory universe of terms alone. For even a judgment about terms is and cannot help but be a judgment about terms as entities, the sign of this being the use, at least implied, of the *copula*. So why not consider the other entities as well, such as the throats without which the sounds cannot be produced, eyes by which the words are seen and so on.

Prescriptivism's most startling aspect, replacement of judgment by decision, is thus a consequence of Hare's lack of metaphysics. A real moral law would be inexplicable, so he has to give us one while pretending to do something else, an ambiguity heralded in the crucial phrase "It is proper". He is led to a dogmatic anti-metaphysics too radical to be consistently maintained. For example, in Hare's example of a moral argument[15] he can only make use of his two principles, viz. universalization and prescriptivity, because he makes a metaphysical assumption, for him unwarranted, of parity of ontological standing among men, such that what B prescribes for A is also applicable to himself in a way that Hare, doubtless, would not consider applicable in an argument between B and, say, a flea about reciprocal rights of elimination.[16] But to admit to this presupposition would be to weaken the air of logical inevitability in his system with which Hare is so pleased.

> If a man wants to escape from my concepts, where is he going to flee to.[17]

Apart from this assumption about equality, there are other indications that Hare's moral philosophy begins *after assuming* the natural law or antecedent moral principles which it goes on to reject. For example, he writes that

> If we can show that there is a form of argument which, without assuming any antecedent moral premisses, but given that people are as they are and the world as it is, will lead them... to agree upon certain moral principles which are conducive to the just reconciliation of conflicting interests, then we shall have done, perhaps, all that is required.[18]

Since a moral notion of justice is assumed this statement of Hare's programme amounts to a denial that he is attempting a complete theory of morals.

---

15 *Freedom and Reason*, chapter 6.

16 He might not even consider it applicable in an argument between B and a child or, perish the thought, between B and a woman. The commitments involved, as to ontological standing, can only be made outside of Hare's theory which thus, in itself, achieves very little. In the issue of race, for example, the argument that one would not oneself like to be discriminated against has no purchase against an opponent who insists that black people are as such incapable of assuming equal responsibilities. The factual question has to be met on its own grounds, just as there is no point in defending women's rights, or those of the foetus, while neglecting to disabuse one's opponent of his belief that women have no souls or that the foetus is not a person. Conversely, one might have to show an animal rights protester that animals have no (rational) souls, are of less worth than humans.

17 *Ibid.* p. 201.

18 *Ibid.* p.185.

But since it is self-contradictory (how show something just without assuming an "antecedent moral" premiss about justice?) it will not even help towards a meta-ethical theory of moral reasoning.

It is indeed simpler and more reasonable to begin one's moral theory with an axiom about justice than with the prescriptivity of moral language.[19] Starting from the latter Hare never succeeds in representing justice adequately, though this appears to be his goal. His Nazis, for instance, can never be proved unjust. They are either argued to be inconsistent, as both willing and unwilling to take their own medicine, or to be fanatics and thus beyond the reach of moral argument. There seems no place for an argument to show that they are unjust, just as there are no antecedent moral principles. What then of the rationality of morals? Hare admits not only to an inability to persuade fanatics (no philosophers have claimed this ability) but also, as if it were the same thing, to an inability to demonstrate their irrationality.[20]

He claims, however, that his concepts are more general and "formal" than those of other moralists. But it is only a virtue to begin with formal (i.e. logical) concepts if one's unargued view of "the world as it is" be correct. We do not get from the formal to the "material" concepts (real moral principles) any more than, for example, the ontological argument gets from the idea to the existence of God. The force of "formal" is in fact negative. It means, not having a reference to reality or, still less, nature. So to begin with formal concepts is to exclude nature and natural law *a priori* and incidentally to deny the rationality of morals since all that we are offered via these formal concepts is an *argumentum ad hominem*[21], i.e. a formal logical fallacy. What was needed here was to remember, or at least understand, that all knowledge begins with the strictly indubitable sense-experience of the "proper sensibles", interpreted intellectually by abstraction and by abstractions performed upon these abstractions, in the way explained by the present author elsewhere[22]. Even these "formal" concepts are thus ultimately derived from a primary experience of material reality.

As for Hare's concepts being more general, in one crucial respect, that of human freedom, they are very particular, as his specimen argument shows. For him a frontal disobedience of conscience is *logically* impossible — a very particular view indeed.

For Hare's premiss here is that moral *language*, and not just the moralist, prescribes, so that when I say "A ought to do X" I am *saying* "Let A do X", an imperative. If, in contrast to this, he says,

---

[19] In fact one should begin with a general study of human acts (and of the end of action), their voluntariness, their goodness and badness and so on.

[20] P. 184.

[21] Chapter 6.

[22] E.g. in *Philosophy or Dialectic?*

> B is using the word "ought" *non*-prescriptively, then "I ought to put A into prison for debt" does not entail the *singular* proposition "Let me put A into prison".

One wants rather to insist that the indicative sentence cannot *entail* the imperative *however* "ought" is used. Imperatives, as analysed here, involve the will, decision, involve "acts" in fact, *actual followings* of the moral judgment. As such they cannot be *part of the language* of morals. If they were then we would be unable to see a difference between deliberate misbehaviour and logical error, or the distinction between action and thought, deep-rooted as this is.

Hare writes further that if B is using "ought" non-prescriptively then "the moral judgment becomes quite irrelevant to the choice of what to do." But one must note here that if, on the other hand, "ought" is used prescriptively then in Hare's system the choice is *already made*, the judgment *is* the choice. All Hare is entitled to mean by "quite irrelevant to" is "logically independent of", not at all the same thing.

If, as it would seem from the account, one cannot knowingly do wrong then one wants to ask how Hare would explain moral evil, a fact, or even moral weakness. The theory cannot explain it, so he has to explain it away. For him what is called moral weakness is no more than a *linguistic* peculiarity:

> If a man does what he says he ought not to, though perfectly able to resist the temptation to do it, then there is something wrong with what he says, as well as with what he does. In the simplest case it is insincerity; he is not saying what he really thinks. In other cases it is self-deception; he thinks that he thinks he ought, but he has escaped his own notice using "ought" in an off-colour way.[23]

The huge counter-example of human moral evil is brushed aside by assertion only. The lengths to which Hare goes to avoid recognizing it are amazing. "What makes the moral life so appallingly difficult", he says, is the difficulty of "finding some action to which one is prepared to commit oneself" and "to accept as exemplifying" a moral principle.[24] This seems unavoidably to mean that he accepts *tailoring* one's moral principles to what one is prepared to do, so that one need never condemn oneself. This though is to accept the mind-set of Macbeth, as perceived by his more clear-sightedly evil wife:

> What thou wouldst highly
> That wouldst thou holily,
> Wouldst not play false
> And yet wouldst wrongly win.[25]

It is arguable that this play shows and was intended to show rather powerfully that such an approach is no preservative, such as even a Freud understood

[23] *Ibid.* p.83.
[24] P.73.
[25] *Macbeth* I,V.

that we needed, against the evil hidden in the heart. In solving the difficulty to his own satisfaction (of finding moral principles not in conflict with previous intentions) Hare contrives to be if anything more radical than Nietzsche while appearing more discreet.

Hare gives it as a point in favour of his theory that in it "ought" implies "can". In fact, we have seen, it implies more. In his scheme it implies "cannot not". By contrast the ordinary moralist's "ought" implies both "can" and "is not forced to". This is proved by an analysis of language far more direct and incontrovertible than Hare's mere hypothesis *about* moral language. For we tell a man that he ought to do something only when we assume both that he is free to do it (i.e. can) and that he is free not to do it (is not compelled), thus allowing in our very use of the word for that moral weakness so fatal to Hare's theory. If one says to himself "I ought to die within seventy years" then in so far as he is not free to abstain from such dying his "ought" *ipso facto* becomes metaphor for "can be expected to". Conversely, "I ought to live for ever" becomes, just in so far as one is not free to do this, a figure of speech for "If someone has the power then *he* ought to enable me to live for ever". Yet if one says "I ought to pay this tax bill" then this change of meaning does not occur, just because one both can pay it and might fail to do so. There is no shred of a reason for saying with Hare that if I in fact fail to fulfil my "ought" or even do not intend to do so then this attitude affects the word's meaning. It has nothing to do with the word.

Where moral weakness is in evidence but explanations in terms of insincerity or "off-colour" word-usage are hopelessly implausible then Hare resorts to theories of physical or psychical powerlessness. He has to do this since, as he says,

> It is a tautology to say that we cannot sincerely assent to a command addressed to ourselves, and *at the same time* not perform it, and it is in our (physical and psychological) power to do so.[26]

"Power" is a vague or ambiguous term. A normal moralist will admit that we do not always seem able to get to the required point of unconditionally wanting to do what we ought. But this is not to deny that "ought" implies "can" since it does not excuse us. We can still do our duty *if we want to* and that is a perfectly good sense of "can". No one says that it is not in a man's power to go shopping for his wife just because he does not and cannot want to do so. The tyrant's not wanting to be just to his victims does not excuse him, as if it were not in his power to be just. Far from a man's heart being in the wrong place excusing him it is just for this that we blame him, just as St. Paul, whom Hare himself cites, blamed himself. He does not, in *Romans* 7, as Hare

[26] *The Language of Morals* p.20, quoted *Freedom and Reason* p.79.

requires, disclaim responsibility for his sins. He would then, like the Manichees of old, have had no reason to trouble himself about them. But men, he says, are "without excuse" (*Romans* 2, 1). So much for appeals to scripture.

Thus Hare's psychological "can't", in any case, is compatible with our normal freedom to do what we sincerely and fully think we ought, unlike the physical "can't". Moral weakness remains as clear refutation of universal prescriptivism. Thus Hare suggests that angels or beings who *by definition* can do no wrong would proceed by his method[27], and exactly that has been our criticism of it, viz. that it does not allow for the evident wrong-doing in the world. His language, however fitting for angels, does not fit human reality.[28]

---

[27] *Ibid.* p.73f.

[28] Hare does not much modify in later work the inital presuppositions discussed here in terms of his first two books, but argues rather "with renewed vigour for many of the conclusions with which he is most closely identified" (Jonathan E. Adler's review in *Mind* XCIX, January 1990, p.131, of Douglas Seanor and N. Fotion, *Hare and Critics: Essays on Moral Thinking*, Oxford 1988). My concern here, as in Kant's case, had to be restricted to certain influential texts in the first instance.

Chapter 9

Ethical Rules or Moral Laws?

We return, after considering the deviations of Kant and Hare, to the basic topics of moral theory, such as the one named in the title above. We might begin by taking note of a typical notice found in the underground railway system of one of the world's cities:

> We don't like prohibitions either, but for the comfort and security of all concerned certain rules are to be observed both on the stations and in the trains.[1]

One might ask, what's the point of that? They are forbidding something, e.g. throwing banana skins around in the carriages;[2] why are they ashamed of it? Their shame shows, at least, that prohibitions are necessary. Prohibitions, of course, are imposed on a man or woman by someone else. This can be true also of a *rule*, but not necessarily. One can impose a rule on oneself.

Now from one point of view the whole of modern ethics has been an attempt to reduce laws to rules, of reason or of thumb, which an individual man or his reason imposes upon himself, even if he should or could be thought to necessarily impose it.

The situation is illustrated further by the futile attempts mentioned earlier to draw up ethical rules, so as to deal, for example, with problems in medical practice, a more complexified practice, clearly, than the smooth management of an underground railway system. I speak of medical practice rather than of medical *ethics*, since it is a question of what is *to be done*, in crisis situations particularly, in the field of medicine and medical care. Yet the idea that this *praxis* might be or even might ever have been carried on without any ethics at all, so that ethical "norms" are then added to it on account of conscientious scruples, is simply incoherent.

Ethical realities are and have to be rooted in the essence of praxis, which is acting for a purpose. What is that purpose? Ultimately it is happiness, fulfilment. The point is almost "analytic" as meaning the attainment of end, the satisfaction of the want motivating pursual of purpose. How though do we get such happiness? Answer: by acting so and not so, and acting so, acting in the right (*recta*: straight) way towards happiness, is what acting morally *means*. There could be no course envisaged which would be called acting morally but which was of no use for human happiness. This being so, happiness itself

---

[1] Stockholm's *tunnelban*.

[2] This was one of the pictorial illustrations accompanying the announcement.

becomes a or the moral value or end and, in Martin Grabmann's words, *höchste Entfaltung der Sittlichkeit*.[3]

So this is not utilitarianism, which was the reduction of morality to a *technical* praxis, an adaptation of means to ends, though giving no analysed account of the end itself, of happiness. The main fault of utilitarianism, however, is that it shifts the burden of calculation to the individual. This is against the *essence* of morality and of moral science, the first principles of which are and have to be supplied by custom, *consuetudo*, as Aristotle taught and which even Hume in his way confirms with his insistence that moral judgments can only be derived, if at all, from antecedent moral judgments. Hence Aristotle can say that a badly brought up person cannot know what is being spoken of in ethics.[4]

This deference to custom may strike us as rather weak, trained as we are in the traditions of the Enlightenment, for which custom and intelligent analysis are the respectively negative and positive poles of a worthy human response to reality. But the rise of the hermeneutic viewpoint can help us to modify this impression. Thinking without previous influences as advocated by Descartes, it is now clear, is impossible. This, again, is the real meaning of Hume's claim that one cannot derive "ought" from "is". In our praxis, inclusive of our practical thinking, we always start from some previous practical principle not at present in doubt, as, for example, revolutionaries appeal and have to appeal to our notions of justice (even Hitler did that). The very foundation of *praxis* itself is a practical principle, viz. good is to be pursued and evil avoided, for good here has the meaning of purpose or end. The principle means, it might be said, aim at something, have ends. But what can be aimed at can only be a good, i.e. something one can will, and here the principle is shown to have metaphysical content, the good being a reality, a being, as presented to the will. To see the principle as an analytical tautology would thus be to misunderstand it. At the same time the principle does not direct that one be a good person in some special moral sense of goodness. Morality comes in with the following of, with the conformity of action with the principle. So if the principle only meant that one do good morally we would have an empty circle, as if one said to another, "Obey this law (i.e. the law which I now enunciate)."

But is there a special moral sense of good at all? We considered this matter earlier. In saying that the only thing in the world which was good without qualification was a good will Kant appeared to believe that he was clarifying the tradition to itself. In fact, and ultimately due to a negative *theological* influence going back to a late-medieval thematization of the idea of the

---

[3] M. Grabmann, *Thomas von Aquin*, Munich 1959.

[4] Utilitarianism might be represented as the mistaking of the metaphysical justification of morals for the supreme rule of praxis. In this process, however, the metaphysics itself gets badly deformed.

absolute power of God, he was making a seminal mistake. What the tradition says, once more, is that, since the will determines in man the use of everything else, it is therefore the goodness of the will as a natural reality (we might even say therefore its *physical* goodness as a faculty, naturally having *ens* become *bonum*[5] for its object) which determines whether the man *qua* man is good, i.e. in his willing and acting. This goodness of man in his willing and acting, i.e. in his *human* acts, is his essential goodness (unlike his goodness as a physical, i.e. material, specimen or as an ice-hockey player), which we call his *moral* goodness. *Calling* it his moral goodness is not changing the simple meaning of the word "goodness", but merely signalling that we are speaking of the goodness of a rational agent as such.

So when we speak of the ethical problems of medical praxis, for example, we should mean the problems as to how that praxis should be conducted as a *human* activity, the techniques being properly human techniques, so as to attain our human ends and end. It is a question, that is, of safeguarding certain transcendent *goods*, not merely of keeping certain rules. Thus Aquinas will write that evil, moral evil, is not finally a matter of disobedience to law but of unsuitability of action to end. So if we say that abortion is never to be permitted we commit ourselves to the view that abortion, or killing an innocent, does not get us to where we want to be, ever. More generally, injustice is a name for what always harms the common good.

A difference from utilitarianism lies in the traditional theory of what a human act is. The intention of the action has to be *first* present in the mind for the action to be performed at all. Thus an action (e.g. a surgical operation) can fail of its object through no fault of the agent and yet have the *same* moral quality as when the intended good is attained. This applies also to acts springing from bad intentions.

The transcendent goods, also called *common* goods, mentioned above, are what principally cause morality to be not fundamentally explainable as a matter of obeying laws, as the stress on duty might have suggested. It is rather a matter of acting practically or for an end. Yet there do exist unbreakable laws of morality.

By common goods we do not mean aggregate goods. There *are* aggregate goods. The more profit a company makes the more each shareholder gets. But human life, or truth-telling, or faithfulness and temperance, are not such goods. We all and each share the *full* common good, but each one cannot himself have all of the company's profits. A man or woman and his or her friend have, though two people, the *same* good of friendship. In this way to intend to cause the death of an innocent, for whatever reason, is contrary to the *common*

[5] It is *ens* as desired which is *bonum*. Really there is only *ens*. *Bonum* is an *ens rationis* (Cf. Aquinas, *De potentia VII*).

good since it makes the good aimed at *alien* to the victim. To seek to cut someone off from our common life betrays the whole of humanity. One might do it to anyone coming innocently into that situation.

Along these lines one can see the sense of absolute prohibitions. But one may still doubt whether they are really *laws*. We may have shown that there are certain types of action which can never be generally justified, such as euthanasia perhaps. But would that really oblige the doctor, when alone with the patient who wants him to kill her, to observe this principle?

In reply one can point to the general insecurity caused if doctors are to permit themselves such secret decisions. This shows how undesirable this would be, but not that it would transgress a law. It will be found, however, that being able to save ourselves from wholesale confusion and ethical disaster will require our taking this last step as well, as the response which reality demands. We will have to admit that the system of ethical principles is in the end a system of laws which we *never* have authority to transgress, save where this is known to accord with the legislator's intention (*epieicheia* as a part of justice). But how can this result, which we either desire or abhor or both, be shown to emerge?

*

*   *

One would want to claim, first, that the moral rules have this legal character; second, that they can only have it if they are given by a divine legislator. Someone who opposes the idea of a divine legislator might still accept that they were laws with binding character, as his conscience tells him, but he would not be able to justify this theoretically.

To say that these moral rules make up the precepts of natural law is to say that they are dictated to us by the exigences of human nature, or, alternatively, that they are clear to us by the natural light of human reason, or, thirdly, that they are *precepts* because that light is the reflected light of the *divine* nature within us. Only this latter can give reason its authority. Thus against a purely Aristotelian rationalism, according to which these laws and the natural inclinations which they mirror give the way to attain our end and perfection, the existentialist can and has objected that he might not want that. Against this line in turn Kant, who defended moral obligation without assigning a functional role to God, has no defence. We may indeed think that the existentialist objection is futile but it is common. Why cannot I sacrifice the future, or even eternity, act like a lunatic, if I so wish? The common liberal defends it as a right.

Here one needs to recall other aspects of the doctrine of natural law, such as its being part of a general theory of law. Aristotle did not divorce ethics from politics, as Kant and Mill have done, at the same time as they lost the understanding of the common good referred to above. For Aristotle, as for a utilitarian, happiness was the ultimate motivation. But this included the happiness, the common good, of society, on the analogy of friendship, which is a good which one friend simply cannot possess on his own. He does not have half of the good of it, but it is common to him and his friend. Yet each individual needs to partake of such a common good for his own happiness. Along these lines one can see how man *needs* the virtues, inclusive of the essentially other-directed virtue of justice, in order to achieve his own happiness. There is no clash between duty and proper love of self, no place for altruism.

So in reading Aristotle or St. Thomas one comes upon passages where the author seems to be referring indifferently and at one and the same time both to moral and to public or statutory law, called *lex humana*. An example is in the discussion, in Aquinas's *Summa theologica*, of *epieicheia* or equity, the virtue of knowing when one should break the letter of the law or the customary rule for the sake of greater fidelity to the legislator's intention.

Now this natural connection between legislation and morals is quite lost in the liberal tradition. Yet it would be easy to show how people's attitudes to abortion, say, in, for example, Sweden, were changed by the law's coming to permit it. Law, that is to say, has a natural teaching function, as Locke stressed, and it is indeed fairly easy to predict that where law does not punish or somehow show disapproval of a given activity, e.g. by making it difficult, there people will tend to think that the activity in question can't be so bad as unaided moral tradition has tended to suggest. One can indeed extend this consideration by asking whether it is natural, natural to human society, for this moral tradition to be thus unaided, given the sociological witness of the majority of historical situations where there has existed what was called in legal and political theory "the spiritual power", a function of which was to reinforce the moral tradition in a more directly pedagogical and principled way than can be achieved by sporadic interventions of the executive. For the executive, at least under the Christian dispensation, was and is considered to have a less than infallible touch in these matters. It belonged to the state's responsibility, in other words, to honour and listen to the spiritual power, thus transmuting and continuing the ancient and virtually universal practice of public sacrifice to the gods, to higher powers enshrining eternal values.

From the natural law point of view the objection against legislating on behalf of morality, seen by the liberal as an at least potential impairment of individual autonomy, only arises at all in the sense that it is not always technically practical. Thus fraud is punishable; but one simply cannot punish all falsehood at the public level, as parents attempt to do with their children. If one extends the example even to Orwell's "thought-crime" (while prescinding from the evil nature of the particular regime which he depicts), then one can ask whether instinctive revulsion against this is not rooted in the monstrosity of any *public* attempt to control thought rather than in a belief that one need never be held responsible for what one thinks, i.e. that there *are* no "thought-crimes". The project is totally impracticable and would manifestly lead to gross injustice, whatever the intention behind it. A more plausible example is prostitution, which even an integralist like St. Augustine thought it unwise for the state to proscribe. Adultery too has been a crime here and there. The point is that in theories other than the liberal any and every genuinely moral transgression can be validly construed as harming the common good, of which the legislator has the care.

In today's actual situation the legislator's main concern seems to be merely to respect conscience as far as possible without creating anarchy or unfair discrimination, e.g. if children were to be denied blood-transfusions at the parents' behest. Suicide is another example, today permitted, but less than thirty years ago a crime (in the United Kingdom). But the principle of respect for conscience in *this* sense often contradicts itself. Thus if one wrote to Mrs. Thatcher's office during her first election campaign requesting her views and intentions concerning abortion one received the reply that it was Party policy to leave this matter to the individual conscience. But that is just what someone who understands abortion or suicide as murder may not do. Such a state can only have a weakened legitimacy in his eyes: in the end the liberal principle, taken further, *qua* principle, than a mere tendency, cannot be upheld.

Thus it is a role of law to form consciences, since, we seem to find, if it neglects to do this then it will *malform* consciences. Hence anyone who leaves any type of murder to a decision of private conscience in some way abets it, is even accessory to it. The right to life of certain groups is not a legitimate matter of controversy and, once conceived, there is no test for being a human being. Throughout life the quality of life is just that, viz. that one is alive.

This rule, of course, does not only apply to murder. If one thought homosexual intercourse wrong one could hardly condone the state's indifference to it, i.e. if one accepted the type of continuity which we are indicating between human and natural, or positive and moral, law. Debate might then better centre round how far we remain bound to traditional sexual morality, round why homosexual intercourse is wrong, if it is, instead of endlessly treading the narrow circle of ideas concerning toleration and enforcement.

Many people feel uncomfortable about following the arguments where they lead here. But silence in the face of unease is unhealthy. Doctors, for example, must be able to pursue concrete ethical discussion and discourse without always being bogged down in see-saw discussions over first principles, which is where liberals tend to wish to deposit ethical problems. Such discussions need not be see-saw, if the participants have metaphysical acumen and a modicum of cultural history at their disposal, but this would only accidentally be the property of a doctor. The layman (lay, from the point of view of moral philosophy) should not be made to feel he has to prove everything, more or less apologize for everything in fact, in the face of an iconoclastic opponent, who is thus given the advantage.[6] As Frank Snare put it, the correct answer to someone demanding further proof before he will follow any moral prescription, of even the most certain kind, would be to forcibly restrain him.[7] The recipe is of course ambiguous, but we would certainly want to respond in this kind of way to someone proposing to kill a speaker at an academic symposium (he pulls out a gun), rather than try to prove to him the error. Nonetheless there are answers to such questions, as supplied by the natural law tradition. But that a religious or theistic view is required is not surprising. If man be not created in God's image then any talk about the sacredness of human life is mere Chauvinism, as Glover and others are not slow to point out. The word "speciesism" is coined, and rights become ridiculed by a pretence of applying them to brutes. A readiness to sterilize those one does not think much of, practiced by the Nazis and legal in Sweden up to the 1970s (thanks largely to materialist socialist ideology) is another case in point. Kant wanted us to treat people as ends, never as means, but he took away all reason for doing so; as Sartre showed, again, his notion of freedom could as well be viewed entirely negatively.

Against this not only do we need to restore the category of natural religion in philosophy to the role which it plays in, say, Cicero's treatment of the laws. We also need to restore the role of religion in public life, whether this be a role played by the Christian churches or by some generalized public deference to religion such as we find in More's *Utopia* in the sixteenth century. In his perfect society More disallowed persecution of people for their honest opinions but still argued that those who denied God or the soul's immortality should be forbidden to propagate their views, since this would destroy respect for and obedience to law. For if God does not exist, says Dostoyevsky's Ivan, then everything is permitted, i.e. one may permit oneself everything *with impunity*. Given that it is always only the few who prefer to be Socrates dissatisfied than a pig satisfied[8], or who prefer justice and honour to ill-gotten gains, this obviously has wide social and cultural consequences.

So here we move further into the political dimension, from which medical ethics, for example, cannot be isolated. In matters of life and death, indeed, to reiterate, few people will be guided by unaided ethical rules and the weak,

[6] This is the attitude behind the claims of moral philosophers such as Torbjörn Tännsjö, who claims that professors of ethics are the ones with competence as to what society ought to do. He himself will tell us that we can abort babies of the "wrong" or undesired sex, for example. A Swedish critic, Alf Svensson, compares Tännsjö to someone who does not realise that the wheel has already been invented, i.e. there are moral certainties.

[7] F. Snare, "Dissolving the Moral Contract", *Philosophy*, July 1977.

[8] This is a much safer assertion than that of Hare that "fanatics will always be few".

where inconvenient, will "go to the wall". We need moral laws, according to which we must sometimes make new human laws. Recent legislation, however, has born more the character of a retreat from law. Yet everything must reflect the eternal law, the reality and order of the world which, it was always thought, gives body to justice. In a Christian society note would thus have to be taken, as it was taken, of what was claimed to be, in addition, a revealed divine law, a great part of which, however, only reaffirmed the eternal and natural law. Under its influence the age-long tide of infanticide, for example, was pushed back to India and China and adjoining territories, as study of the acts and speeches of the first ecclesiastics in northern Europe, or in Rome itself, can show. It is about these things that ethically concerned people will in future have to argue and at times fight.[9]

*

* *

There is a lot of confusion about conscience. In the order of explanation conscience comes perhaps first. "In the depths of his conscience man discovers a law", proclaims a modern church document.[10] But the praxis which this law dictates is not itself in the first place the following of conscience, but the following of this law "which man does not give to himself". The specific duty to follow conscience (even though we discover this law in conscience) is such a secondary part of this law that many moral codes do not even mention it. In other words, to do what one thinks is right is only a part of doing what is right as such.

This means, negatively, that one always does wrong if one disobeys conscience. But it does not mean that one always avoids wrongdoing by obeying conscience. Even in the case of an *invincible* ignorance what a man does remains *materially* sinful, even though he be excused, though it is an old maxim that we are obliged to know the law. Errors of conscience are often due to previous neglect of the duty to seek truth and goodness.

Believing that following conscience is our *first* duty distorts our consciences, since then we fail to see that even in our *own* judgments of conscience we are appealing to a higher authority, not just making a private *decision* of principle. Thus doctors in England who said that their consciences did not permit them to help with abortions were told by state authorities that they still had a duty to tell their patients where they *could* go to get abortions. But

[9] An interesting corollary is that the state has to promote what is noble in man, as alone tending to preserve a coherent society. Even when democratically elected (and this is itself a noble principle) the state will be aristocratic in character, as promoting what is spontaneously followed only by the few who need no law.

[10] Vatican II (1962-1964), *Gaudium et Spes* 16.

obviously this is just as wrong. These doctors were not just privately opting out. Rather, they would have no choice but to condemn the law in the name of natural law, at once eternal and divine. The state was treating them like "conscientious objectors" who, as we say, just do not want to get their hands dirty. But we should not say that, should not blind ourselves to the condemnation implied in the dissenters' dissent. Where it is made explicit little is affected, though it becomes less possible to marginalize the objector. A priest in West Germany who declared that abortionists at a local clinic were murderers was imprisoned by the local magistrate. Conscience, anyhow, of its nature witnesses to a higher authority. "In this way man has a law written by God in his or her heart, which it belongs to his dignity to obey." Hence a Catholic, for example, cannot *as such* oppose conscience to the authority instructing him. The authority itself determines where conscientious objection is allowed.[11] All appeal is to law and conscience is reason's act of recognition of law, not some *sui generis* impulse.

*

* *

The Australian philosopher mentioned above who recommended resort to force with cessation of dialogue against those who challenge morality argued from a *contractualist* theory of it. According to this primitive human beings made a contract to observe certain rules, which became morality. Now even if one stops short of interpreting this little tale historically it will always postulate an ontological priority of human nature over these moral rules and hence a separation of it from morality. This is contractualism's basic error. Such a background makes possible the utilitarian attitudes with which we are familiar, whereby one *opposes* ethical scruples with what is practical and feasible. The specious strictness of Kantianism, which in the end leads to blind and shameless laxity, is filled with the same error. In fact, however, the ethical is the very essence of the practical, evil being explained, as we found Aquinas saying, not as disobedience to law, ultimately, but as unsuitability of action to end. This though is because law itself is explained in this way, as a rational ordering for some end, often as a condition for explaining it, so that if one fails to obey one will not attain the end and *this* alone is what makes the disobedience wrong.

Here Aquinas differed from the fourteenth century theologians and their Lutheran successors who took as their ultimate category the absolute power of

[11] This is of course also the claim of the state, which, however, finds itself in a weaker position intellectually through not being able to lay claim to any infallibility. It makes up for this, however, by the instruments of physical compulsion and punishment. Furthermore, we are by nature subjects of the state, whereas we are members of such a church only by a choice in principle our own.

God. Aquinas might have said, God obliges us to pursue our end under pain of not attaining it if we do not pursue it. Such an obligation could attach to any end once chosen. What is meant, however, is that there *is* some one ultimate end of human life, to resist which will entail destruction in our very essence.

Here alone it is that the precepts appear as precepts, to which our obedience is due whatever we may think. This though is our religious duty, and it belongs to justice to obey God, as one might see even hypothetically. To this extent the later theologians were right. But they were wrong to emphasise divine sovereignty at the expense of divine wisdom.

Thus in moral philosophy one often refers to the question raised in Plato's *Euthyphro*, viz. is a thing right because God (sc. the gods) commands it, or does God command it because it is right? It often seems self-evident to those who once raise this question that the latter is the true answer, as the only alternative to a degenerate theological positivism. This is not, however, Aquinas's answer and, in fact, it lacks metaphysical insight. One must do justice to both sides of this matter. So Aquinas declares that it is only in human law that something is forbidden because it is bad and not bad because it is forbidden;

> but if it be referred to the natural law, which is contained firstly, indeed, in the eternal law, but secondarily in the natural power of judgment of human reason, then every sin is evil because it is prohibited.[12]

How can this be? It is so, ultimately, because law and goodness depend upon the divine *being*, on how God is. It would be impossible for the latter to depend upon the former; the goodness which the Platonists posited as prior to being can only be the goodness of the unique divine being itself, defined as cause of all else. This being is the being which cannot be determined by anything higher. Thus God can indeed command us as he wishes. Hence our ethical response has to include an obedience beyond our personal insight. This is the natural way to *improve* our insight (as faith is said to improve understanding).

This suggests, it even means, that there must always be deference to the existing moral tradition and customs, as starting-points at least. Thus moral conscience does not exist in a vacuum, but is formed by parents and educators, being in *this* way the promulgation to us of natural law. It would appear indeed that the main error of utilitarianism is its deliberate disregard of whatever falls outside the calculation of the *individual* agent.

What we say here has implications for the relation of philosophy itself to theology and to tradition, just as it has political implications. Disregard of natural law naturally brings disasters. Rightly understood the point is analytic. The disasters of the last times, in which Christians believe themselves to live,

---

[12] Aquinas, *Summa theologica* Ia-IIae 71, 6 ad 4um.

might seem to be upon us in the train of an unprecedentedly canonized rejection of tradition. Thus many would trace the plague of modern total war to a gradual acceptance of usury, or the plague of AIDS to the discrediting of traditional sex morality. Others, of course, will put the latter down to insufficient prophylaxis merely. But in any event the case is strong, as argued earlier in this book, for saying that the problems of medical ethics, whether of theory or of praxis, will not be solved until the civil power again has recourse to spiritual authority, which, says St. Paul, "judges all things".

*

* *

The doctrine of natural law is just one very important instance of the teleological principle that *omnis agens agit propter finem*, every agent acts for an end. This principle need not be confined to rational agents; it can be applied to everything that happens, though one is then saying, or implying, that order, any order, requires an ordering intelligence, the major premise of Aquinas's Fifth Way of knowing that God exists.

Hence to be consistent one cannot defend natural law without committing oneself to a generally teleological philosophy of nature. One should not fear, in face of the mechanistic tradition of natural science, that this is too difficult. Such a fear has led some defenders of natural law to develop non-traditional doctrines which represent natural law in name alone, a deception to which their loyalty to an ecclesiastical tradition appears to blind them. This ploy was not necessary; the work of rehabilitating teleology in the philosophy of natural science proceeds apace, while the mechanist alternative is anyhow now far less plausible than it seemed to many in the nineteenth century. It is time really for those who live on and from the classical heritage to go on to the offensive.[13]

[13] See our *The Recovery of Purpose* (Peter Lang, Frankfurt 1993), Chapter IX, for an analysis of the situation.

Chapter 10

The Impossibility of Altruism

Here we shall discuss more thematically those objections which we have been urging against the idea of altruism. First of all, though, we should consider that if altruism is indeed impossible, incoherent indeed, then some explanation for its wide acceptance as a kind of moral paradigm seems necessary. For the altruism with which we are familiar is typically secularist, yet it has, and can only have, religious roots. The same applies to the altruism found in the ancient world. Secondly, altruism as we know it could not get off the ground, we shall show, without a voluntarist theory of willing which is itself indefensible. This consideration, however, situates altruism within a culturally conditioned historical development of fundamental notions and so it is not really separable from the preceding approach. Related to both of them, in any case, is a puzzle as to the priorities concerning inclination and duty. It will be found that these two are not so much antithetical, as post-Kantian altruism virtually assumes, as at different levels. Inclination is presupposed to duty, which can only itself be explained in terms of our profoundest inclination.

*

* *

At the root of any moral theory which one could call altruistic one would expect to find a separation of the motive of the subject's happiness from the motive of right-doing. Although on the religious view, certainly on the Jewish or Christian view, such a divorce is ultimately impossible (I would argue that it is so on *any* view) it can all the same be shown that the emergence of altruistic theories in modern times is a distorted secularist echo of the very nerve of Biblical tradition.

For this nerve is the total love of God, set forth in Exodus and Deuteronomy and reaffirmed in the Gospels, which corresponds, moreover, to the first precept of the Decalogue, being thus by implication a natural norm like honesty, filial piety or justice itself. Thus it is a norm to be defended by reason's natural powers.

Now the proposal of such a love certainly implies at one level, as *amor amicitiae* or love of friendship, a renunciation of one's own happiness as and when the divine will should require it. But the religious tradition would no longer be itself without the confidence that such a disposition is *always* the way to human fulfilment[1] at the final level, where of course happiness belongs. What distinguishes this view is the distance at which it places this level from more mundane purviews, leading it to recommend a certain forgetfulness of happiness which at least puts one in mind of altruism. "He who seeks to save his life will lose it."

To this, however, there is added

> He who loses his life for my sake and the Gospel's will keep it unto life eternal,

Christ being the speaker. Such motivation, of life eternal, excludes altruism, though not, as is sometimes claimed, selfless love. For the fact that selfless love pays in the end is the only thing that, in the end, can demonstrate its rightness. When the prophet Daniel and his friends declared that perhaps God would deliver them if the heathen king tormented them for keeping the divine law, but that even if he did not they would still keep it, then the intention of the text is clearly to preserve the idea that God rewards those who keep his law while fixing it at a certain logical and ethical distance from the motivation for so acting. The cause of such a distance, however, is not some kind of analytical dichotomy between the two concepts of duty and reward. It is caused, rather, by the immanent logic of love and trust, such that we do not have to concern ourselves about the response of the beloved to our service, in which, moreover, there is a certain gladness to be found as in the doing of "our bounden duty", as in keeping a pledge to a friend or pleasing a father.

Selflessness, in fact, cannot but have its reward because this reward, this happiness, remains internal to the life of virtue, of selflessness, understood as living according to God (*vivere secundum Deum*), whom as goodness (*bonum in communi*) all desire. That the reward, paradoxically perhaps, increases in proportion as it is not looked towards is to be explained in terms of the nature of spiritual reality which is, again, equated with love. Thus in Catholic teaching on penance perfect sorrow for sin is that sorrow which is motivated solely by thought of the divine goodness and no longer by fear of condemnation, commendable as such imperfect sorrow may be. The lover, we may add, finds himself in losing himself because he is not ontologically a material unit defined by the limits of his extension as against others. He is rather a *person* whose actualized being consists in his relationships. His being is to give himself away. As Aquinas said of God, quoting Dionysius, goodness is diffusive of itself (*bonum est diffusivum sui*), while Augustine gives as motive for creation, "we exist because God is good". Love, and not duty, is the essence of

[1] In a *bonum commune* or common good of friendship, even if with God alone, which Aquinas argues suffices for happiness. Such individual salvation, however, is not an egoistic possession of good but precisely a sharing in this common good of divine friendship. The presence of other, human friends, however, is appropriate to this blessed state (Cf. *Summa theol.* Ia-IIae 4, 8).

that goodness which the moral law would enshrine. Duty needs love to make sense of itself.

Altruism, however, tries to import these perspectives, which we may justly call transcendental, into a secularist and materialist world view. The result is an irreconcilable conflict between the natural hope of happiness and the demands of our moral nature, with *no* motivation given for following the latter, motivation itself, after all, being a matter of the agent's hope of happiness. I am motivated, that is, by what I want or lack and to have got what I want, without further want, is to be happy. Thus even if altruism could be shown to be in some respects reasonable, or even demanded by reason, yet no motive could be offered for being reasonable in this way. In a transferred sense reason would have been shown to be itself unreasonable, an aberration on the evolutionary landscape.[2]

For such a dualism entails a permanent frustration of human hopes which can only serve to bring virtue into contempt. Some kind of hope, in other words, is internal to virtue. It is the denial of this which makes of altruism, if fully worked out, a radical evil. It has, for example, inspired secularist ideologies, whether of universal or of national socialism (or of "socialism in one country"), which demand the *total* sacrifice of all the human person's aspirations. No fulfilment is possible there.

Total love of God, on the other hand, can be shown to fulfil the human person whose being is premissed to be an image of God, though this is at least equally a total sacrifice (something which illustrates that destruction is not what this term most essentially signifies). A thing and its image are not two objects *between* which one chooses. To love the image as what it is, an image, is to love it for the sake of the original. This is to say that to love God is man's true way of loving himself.[3] In this way the religious person can seek happiness *in* transcending it, which is probably what the well-intentioned altruist thinks he is doing and may be doing in some hidden way. Our point here is merely that he cannot spell it out so as to present a coherent ethical *theory*.

The fact that hope, which *means* hope of happiness, is internal to virtue follows from the platitude, again, that it is of the nature of a precept to be imposed for some end. To obey a precept, follow a dictate of virtue, meaningfully, i.e. in a virtuous way, I must at least believe that there is some good reason for it, whether or not I know what it is. Otherwise I am merely aping the moral posture. For the same reason, to demand that a precept have some end is quite compatible with respect for its preceptedness as such. I do not, for

[2] Cf. J. Montmarquet, "Nagel on Motivation", *Australasian Journal of Philosophy*, March 1982.

[3] In saying "not my will but thine be done" the lover follows his own *deepest* will, as the deed alone will prove.

example, need to be sure that the good end is to my own personal benefit in the first instance. The egoism of such a demand would not be compatible with respect for the law *qua* law, as is the more modest hope that compliance will not generally go unrewarded. But if this is so then we need to show that to recognize a duty transcending most other personal inclinations, although these be the founts of the natural law itself, would yet itself be "according to the order of the natural inclinations", would itself belong to the set of our inclinations.[4] Recognition of duty is in fact a response to our fundamental inclination to act according to reason, this being only explicable as a root inclination on the hypothesis that the human intellect, seat of the rational power, is itself, in Aristotelian terms, the *form* of human nature. We are of course inclined to act according to our own form, our own nature, that which naturally steers and interprets all our senses.

Certainly if duty did not transcend all the other inclinations, apart from the controlling inclination to *bonum in communi* and the controlling precept of love, viz. *bonum est persequendum*, then, as Kant was right to stress, it would not be duty. The point is, though, that it *is* an inclination, a central pillar in the project of human self-fulfilment.[5] This remains true even upon a view of life in which death would end everything. For it is never clear that one must want to prolong life at all costs. An earlier death in pursuit of duty is easily seen as yielding greater satisfaction than a dishonourable alternative, just as people often *prefer* not to be kept alive after ruinous accidents, whatever their eschatalogical beliefs.

This too, as far as it goes, is compatible with St. Paul's saying "If Christ be not raised (sc. from the dead) then let us eat, drink and be merry, for tomorrow we die."[6] For what is pointed to there is not the folly of selfless duty but, rather, the more general pointlessness of human endeavour without at least some implicit hope of eternal life. He would mean, rather, that the man devoted to duty shows forth, whatever he says, a hope of eternal life.[7]

---

[4] Cf. Aquinas, *op. cit.* Ia-IIae 94, 2.

[5] In the identification of good with being Thomist metaphysics frees this argumentation from any taint of abstract moralism. It is reality, and hence the perfection of being, of one's own being, that is pursued, that is, *in other words*, the natural object of the will. Considered as such, reality becomes that *ens rationis* which we call the good (cf. Aquinas QD *De potentia* 7). It is as much for this reason, philosophically, that we can see that reality is the same as "He who is" (Aquinas's Fourth Way) as it is that the identity of the divine goodness and being would follow from that revelation to Moses theologically considered.

[6] *I Corinthians* 15.

[7] A discussion of the tenor of the Pauline corpus as a whole (especially of his view of the moral teachings of the Jewish scriptures) would be needed to support this interpretation of the quoted passage beyond doubt. But he is of course referring in the first place to the ascetic mode of life of a spiritual man viewing the invisible and the eternal, rather than to moral law. Yet the passage remains relevant given that on the religious view moral and spiritual life are continuous with one another (see our *The Recovery of Purpose*, chapter five, with the references to Abbot Cassian).

So it is not said that duty is pointless unless it is rewarded and even done for a reward, but that in a world bounded by death the "dark wind blowing from the future"[8] cancels out any good that might be aimed at apart from immediate sensual and aesthetic satisfactions *which would then become the criteria for virtue and vice*. But they are manifestly not this and the art of Camus, when he tried to show this, paradoxically demonstrated the opposite, because of the virtue, the devotion to truth, which shone forth in his art.

The argument is that disregard or denial of spiritual goods as *ends* of the virtues would compel us to evaluations of behaviour which would frustrate our nature as moral beings by bidding us despair of hopes which are actually constitutive of that moral nature, those inclinations to virtue and measured, rational activity. Hence there is no place for altruism. What is also implied, as Plato saw, is the reality of the spiritual substantial soul in man as fundament of his worth. Such a soul, Aquinas made clear, is a necessary, i.e. an eternal being.

If, in fine, it is a part of virtue itself to hope for a reward then this hope is not an extrinsic motive. Such a love of and desire for the fullness of life is itself virtuous, while it is vicious to "hate one's own soul". What belongs to the virtuous act is *ipso facto* not an admixture sullying its purity.

*

* *

If, in a sense, we have so far focussed upon the cultural roots of altruism then we might now try to exorcize, even excise, it at its *logical* roots, referring back to much that we have said in previous chapters. Logic itself, however, has a cultural history, and so we will find that these roots, of a distorted logical science, in fact lie in the empiricistic notion of the will which is best called voluntarism. This notion is merely the absolutization of the common-sense notion of freedom as freedom from constraint, a notion which common sense tends to treat in a materialistic way, ignoring the danger of a confusion of what is free, something of value, with what is valueless because random. So the insoluble problem which Hare, again, sets himself in *Freedom and Reason*, as the title indicates, is this: how can man be free without rejecting the constraints of reason? As he poses the problem it is indeed insoluble, so that one of the contestants will have to retire. Naturally this will be reason, which is in fact retained in name alone, apart from a requirement of consistency. Anything goes for Hare, even Nazism, provided that one is prepared to follow it through and submit to one's own wilful prescriptions.

---

[8] Cf. A. Camus, *The Outsider* (orig. Fr. *L'Étranger*).

Such a result[9] ought to suggest to us that there is something wrong with the idea that reason constrains. Few people regard it as necessary to freedom to be able to theorize that three threes are eight, or feel enslaved by the requirement that they be nine, though the immature often like to insist on their right to *say*, perhaps even to believe, that three threes are eight. Yet belief does not lie in the power of the will, though they may wish it to do so and though Luther, under the sway of voluntarism, sometimes spoke as if it did. Saying, however, is a practical act and not as such an exercise of theoretical reason.

Does *practical* reason, then, constrain? Does it leave me free, say, to lie? Certainly I am not physically constrained not to lie, or to tell the truth, or to abstain from theft, though reason *forbid* this and might thus be *called* a constraint. Hare and Kant would have it that it is up to me whether to bind myself to these moral rules or not, that I am the legislative authority ("So act that *thou* canst will…", writes Kant). But just as I am not bound to these rules by anything outside myself, so equally I am not bound to the pursuit of happiness and hence, they think, altruism is possible. This is the link with voluntarism, that the freedom which all agree is necessary means a freedom from whatever can be plausibly *called* a constraint, as reason can.

But whatever we call it, reason may no more *be* a constraint than Good Friday is a good Friday. Metaphor and, still more, analogy must be allowed for. In reality the precepts of practical reason, of the natural law, are only accidentally constraints. Primarily they are principles structuring a possible pattern of action. If there were no pattern at all then there would be no actions in the sense of *actus humani*, freely and rationally chosen. Thus the first precept, *bonum est persequendum et malum evitandum*, is wholly positive, requiring activity in pursuit of an end, i.e. activity as such, with, it might almost go without saying, avoidance of what leads away from the end.

The rest of the precepts are then built up, by reason, from a consideration of our nature and its requirements. The possibility of such a derivation is denied by the voluntarists, who say that we are not constrained by our nature. Yet they have no means of justifying the requirement of freedom itself, that we *should* be free, unless this is required by human nature. Sartre, of course, does not justify it. For him it is a burden, a lack in our nature which rather binds than frees.

In natural law theory the ultimate end of all activity is taken to be happiness, with respect to which the will is not free. But this is not taken as a limitation on willing since the concept of freedom, it is thought, is as categorically inappropriate to natural ends as it is to arithmetic.

---

[9] It is no different, however, from the voluntarism of Kant's philosophy. He pretends that one cannot will vicious activity as a universal law, as Hare pretends that "fanatics will always be few". When were they ever?

The voluntarist, indeed, may go on to place his happiness in any "plan of life" he chooses though, as we are stressing, he would not be bound to make his happiness his exclusive or final end at all. So Kant, and followers such as Donagan, argue, against all grammar, that human beings are themselves equally ends, which is identically the formula for altruism.

How one chooses between happiness and the equally ultimate demands of another man or woman altruism is unable to say, nor can it say, outside of the puerilities of the utilitarian calculus, when or to what extent either of the two motivations shall predominate. Yet all attempts to state the altruist's dilemma can only reduce to the unremitting quest for personal happiness (as the most loving of men spoke of his joy being fulfilled), a project though which altruists regard with disdain as tantamount to reason's being the slave of the passions, as they say. To this one may reply that all motivation, as distinct from simply having reasons for one's actions, is a matter of the passions. There is nothing wrong with the passions. I have good reason to step out of the way of an oncoming car, but unless I want to live I have no motive for being thus reasonable. Any *exercise*, even of reason, must come from desire.

Here though the voluntarist fails to advert to the internal connection between intellect and rational appetite. In theoretical reason, for example, it is the unconditioned nature of judgment as such, the fact that it is not determined by organic limitations but aspires to reflect reality, as is proven by the existence of language, of words not tied to particulars, which *is* freedom. Freedom follows from reason's *spirituality*. If it is in its essence already freedom from constraint then it cannot be a constraint. This is why it is wrong to portray the laws of practical reason, not a separate faculty after all but an extension of reason itself to activity, as a set of constraints. The voluntarist is captive to a picture of intellect and will as two marionettes who have nothing in them to show how they came together so neatly in one integral human nature. That the will is itself an inclination *of the mind* seems far less arbitrary even initially.

One has often in philosophy to labour the obvious. If we consider ordinary decision-making, for example, we find it consists in a self-examination as to what one most wants, only intelligible in terms of wanting to be happy. Whatever plan of life one has chosen exists in function of that, as does the most complete sacrifice.

The position of the altruist is arrived at through a somewhat heady, indeed wrong-headed, exaltation of freedom above all natural human ends. He is thus obliged to explain duties to others in the altruistic manner. For he cannot admit to himself the motivation which, at the same time as he wants to deny his natural teleologies as enslaving, he yet wishes to have for being a decent person (or being thought one) except by taking up the largely nonsensical, even ungrammatical story about other people being ends. What is not a means, e.g.

the planet Mars, is not *thereby* an end. It is not an end even if it *ought* not to be somehow made into a means.

Such people end up, inevitably, in an idolization of duty, of "you must because you must". For they have no viable answer to the question why one must, the meaningfulness of which they naturally go on to deny (Prichard), even suggesting that those who ask it are ethically insensitive or wicked (Winch). They blur the distinction between a practical disagreement and an academical discussion about the meaning of the practical.

For one may be ready to grant that the knowledge that something is a duty is a deliberation-stopper, but still want to know, without any necessary implication of wavering in one's duty, why that particular action is a duty and even what the logical and metaphysical conditions are for the existence of duty at all. The deontologists, however, as they are prone to label themselves, have some notion that duty is a prime datum of human nature, rather as we say the ultimate end of happiness is such a datum. Let us see how these two candidates for primitiveness might relate to each other.

*

* *

Happiness, whatever else it may be, is always a matter of getting what one wants, of enjoying. Now in a very ordinary sense of wanting I want to do what I do by the very fact that I do it. Otherwise I would not do it. Nothing is gained by calling this sense of wanting "degenerate" (Donagan) if it is in fact fundamental. It is fundamental to what one means in claiming that anything done for its own sake is also, or, rather, *ipso facto*, done for the sake of happiness, of doing what one wants (to do). It is to be expected that language in practical life is not going to be explicit about what is fundamental to the being of such practical life, and hence we speak of doing for its own sake what is done directly for the sake of the ultimate end. I do it because I like it, we say, and so to do something *literally* for its own sake, and not because we liked it, would be nonsensical, except in the case of some ultimate activity which would give our generalized liking its very *ratio* or essence. Such, indeed, is the ancient theory of contemplation as a participation in the beatific vision, alone desirable *propter se*. One simply could not see God, one with *bonum in communi*, without liking it, since all liking is itself an effect and echo of that being.

Even the most pure observer of duty wants to do his duty. If though he wants it because it is, in turn, his duty to want it then he also wants that further duty, to want to want to do his duty. The wanting must be one step ahead if duty is ever to be actually done.

Why, though, should someone want to do his duty? Even if this is all that he wants he does not escape what in his own eyes is perhaps the *stricture* that he is acting for the sake of happiness since he is doing what he wants. But granted this, is he doing what he wants (his duty) because it is what he wants or because it is his duty? It is useful here to remember the root sense of wanting as lacking. If I lack something then it is in some sense *due* to me, rather as duty is due from me. Hence it can be thought due *to* me that I do my duty. The notion of desire adds little conceptually to that of lack. I can indeed fail to desire something that I lack, but I cannot fail to lack what I desire. So I may lack the giving of justice to a neighbour, but only desire for that will cause me to remedy the lack. This was our point about motivation. No one is going to follow duty unless he wants to. The *rectitudo voluntatis* is only *servata propter se* (Anselm's definition of *iustitia*) when someone wants to observe it *propter se*.

This relates though to the *decision* to follow duty, in the order of exercise as Maritain would say. Can I not, though, make the deliberative *judgment* that duty is to be done (in the order of specification) without in the least wanting to do it? Of course. The question here, however, as it now appears, is whether we can take as the first law of praxis that some purpose or other is to be worked towards and then identify that purpose as duty, or whether we should rather make duty prior and say that it is our duty to have some purpose or other.

These are not the only alternatives. For if we do identify our purpose as duty we *ipso facto* grant that there might be other purposes. The position would remain that there was an anterior or more general law that a purpose is to be aimed at. If this is a *law*, however, then it has itself something of the character of a duty. We might then want to say that it is our duty to have other purposes besides duty, such as to tend wholly to our ultimate end of happiness, to which all other duties must be subordinated, whether as means or in some other way, e.g. participation. They must not be independent of it. That is, the man who in a teleological spirit eschews altruism to that extent acts rightly, however much he may go otherwise wrong in falsely identifying his ultimate end with riches or pleasure or power, say.

The position remains, though, that in doing duty we want to do it, and when we judge that duty is to be done then we judge this as consequence of an unspoken antecedent, viz. if we are to do what we want to do, if we are to be happy. In that "is to be done" lies the unspoken possibility that we can fail to attain our end through not doing our duty, since the analysis shows that end-directedness is *internal* to the concept of "is to be done", the concept, that is, of obligation. It shows, too, as a corollary, that the formally grammatical gerundive form depends upon an assumption of human freedom in those using the language. Precepts, anyhow, are imposed for some end and we are not going to accept the fiction of other people as ends (or any other of Kant's "practical postulates"). The idea that we have to suppose immortality for moral living without being genuinely convinced of its truth is surely a prime case of "having one's cake and eating it". The agony behind it, however, suffused much of the succeeding century's ethical thought, as our next chapter will illustrate.

We could not say of the activity of fulfilling purposes, as we could of that of performing duties, that it was "just one of the things we wanted to do". For all action is defined as for a purpose, i.e. the purpose of the agent, in addition to the object of any action considered in itself (in the order of specification even). Hence the beneficiary of my action cannot himself be its purpose, cannot be an end; *my* purpose, what I want, is to benefit him. I do not want him. Indeed if an end is an end possessed then we would seem to fail in respect for others if we were to treat them as ends.[10] What we should desire, indeed, as end is a union in friendship (on a scale between civic friendship and love) in enjoyment of the common good, a first step towards which, *as means* or as preliminary participation in this end, will be respect for the other's conscience, i.e. for his personal autonomy.

So, anyhow, it is because I want something or other, tend to happiness in other words, that I make any practical judgments at all. Hence it is wrong to speak without qualification of "rational deliberation, which calls in question what the end shall be."[11] Reason, meaning the reasoning man, can have its own natural end, and if freedom not in a subject is merely an abstraction then the nature of the subject does not *qua* nature militate against freedom, though it may do it as a *material* nature. A river, after all, would not be more of a river without banks.[12] That reasoning men can be said, in Donagan's "degenerate" sense, always to do what they most want shows also that wanting itself can be rational and not mere drive or passion, or else it would show that men never act rationally, which is absurd. To be committed to goodness as such is of the essence of rationality (as even Milton's Satan acknowledged in saying "Evil, be thou my good", a serious proposal if ever there was one).

If then I cannot help making practical judgments, so neither can I help wanting to be happy. It is only because of that want that practical reason comes into

---

[10] Kant would say that they were not ends *of ours* (or of anyone's), thus moving further into grammatical nonsense, though he must want to say that each person is an end for him or herself alone. This though seems more a recipe for egoism than for altruism, though the egoism be tempered by an imperative to respect others for as long as I myself wish to be respected, i.e. as unexploitable. Or he might mean that persons are ends in the sense of terminations, merely, in chains of practical reasoning. In any case the programme could only include trying to make others happy if we ourselves wanted this, in itself and from others, which at once brings the real end back into focus, the end, that is, in virtue of which alone one could ever want or will something to be a universal law.

[11] Donagan, *op. cit.* p.231.

[12] Cf. Aquinas, *op. cit.* Ia-IIae 10, 1. "The principle of voluntary motions has to be something naturally willed (as all those things which are not present in something of themselves are reduced to something which is *per se* present). But this is the good as such, the perfect good (*bonum in communi*), to which the will naturally tends as does any power to its object. It is also the last end itself... and all those things which belong to the man willing according to his own nature."

operation at all. If I merely look at the *conception* of duty and declare that it has nothing in common with the *conception* of purpose, the same being true for that matter of any pair of "clear and distinct" conceptions, then I have not yet begun to reason practically. But neither have I said anything at all relevant to practical reason unless I make that declaration, or declare that *iustitia* is *rectitudo voluntatis servata propter se*, *after* I have conceded the constitutive teleological principle of practical reason, viz. *omnis agens agit propter finem*. That is, there is no question of duty for duty's sake being an *alternative* to teleology or to a so-called "mixed" ethic. It comes into play precisely *as* a purpose to be adopted.

It is, however, a purpose which we *should* adopt, good moral living being part of the achieving (*adeptio*) in time of that ultimate aim, beatitude, which, as Grabmann says, again, is not hoped for as part of some utilitarian programme but is itself "the highest development of morality". For since happiness and the hope of it belong themselves to the *ratio* of law it does not derogate from the dignity and authority of law, as we made clear in our chapter on Kant, to take sovereign account of such happiness.

Besides which, however, we *should* also adopt purposes in general, though we cannot help it. This, however, is inseparable from our existence as rational beings and therefore only analogously a duty as the term is normally used.[13]

*

* *

Thomas Nagel's claim[14] that reasons for acting are "objective", i.e. bear first upon someone rather than upon me or you, is, it now seems, not to the point, the point, that is, of acting *for an end*. There might indeed be a reason for acting without one's having a motive. For that it is a *formal* characteristic of reason to universalize does not supply a motive for personal, real action. But without motive no action will be performed. Here we have Hare's mistake in *Freedom and Reason* where, in his debtor's argument, B is not just morally obliged but as it were logically forced to want to be imprisoned for as long as he judges that he ought to imprison A. Yet wants, like motives, are not subject to logic. This does not mean that they cannot be necessary. This was the voluntarist error. They can arise from necessities of nature, "given that things are as they are" as Hare himself, *malgré lui*, somewhere says.

Nonetheless, that reason universalizes in this way can still supply the clue to something further which *can* be a motive, viz. the attainment of universal good, satiating the will.

---

[13] Metaphysically, however, duty is just one instance of created beings fulfilling the eternal law in accordance with the divine government of the world.

[14] T. Nagel, *The Possibility of Altruism*, Oxford 1970.

What does it mean, indeed, for something to act as a motive unless that it promises to satisfy the agent's desires? In this way the objective, universalizing nature of reason itself shows something about *our* nature. For "it is this man that thinks" (Aquinas). We *see* that we should act in certain regular ways. Awareness of this "should" is either of binding law or, many argue, of a generalized rule of self-interest. In either case we can know that not fulfilling the law or rule will harm us. If motive is a matter of desire or attraction, something we want, as we also want to avoid evil befalling us, then we are motivated to obey this law either by fear or by love as passions of the soul.

Nagel doubts whether pure altruism exists or is common. In fact it is impossible. There is a common finality to human action in general, viz. the striving for happiness. Altruism is a recipe for joyless or priggish conventionalism, involving one in a failure to rationally justify what becomes *ipso facto* a mere appearance of rational behaviour and, indeed, a mere appearance of altruism, motivation for which can be left to psychologists to decipher. Thus, as we have said, until present delight be fully operative all virtue is practised under the sign of hope.

Chapter 11

Variations on the Theme

I referred to the torments of the nineteenth century. A representative study, for the English-speaking world, was the book *Liberty, Equality, Fraternity*, by Mr. Justice James F. Stephen.[1] As the title shows, the argument of the book bears a relation to the seismic events in France of less than a century before, in relation to which Stephen adopts a conservative viewpoint, linking him to Burke's *Reflections on the Revolution in France* of 1790 as to de Tocqueville's *Democracy in America* (1830). Stephen, however, has had the advantage of seeing the new ideas further unfold, e.g. in J.S. Mill's moral and political philosophy, and also of witnessing their being tested out.

Much of the discussion of morals in his book, therefore, is in the context of utilitarianism, a form of which Stephen himself defends. He has, however, a very wide notion of it, as may be seen in the last sentence of the "Note on Utilitarianism" with which he concludes his book:

> Now the questions whether we ought to believe in God and in a future state are questions of fact and evidence, and thus the truth of the utilitarian system is proved, for it is shown that the rightness of an action depends ultimately upon the conclusions at which men may arrive as to matters of fact.[2]

This is only shown, of course, if one has accepted Stephen's view that belief in God and a future state is relevant to the question of what moral principles one will assent to, as, we noted, for Thomas More those beliefs were relevant to one's degree of respect for the law, this being a more modest claim than Stephen's.

As the quotation would indicate, Stephen's utilitarianism is not much more than the expression of his rejection of any form of *a priori* intuitionism. It is not so much though, for him, that the latter may be false as that it is not to the purpose, does not account for moral principles in so far as one understands such principles to have binding force. For the intuitionist can give no reason why one should not blunt one's conscience, one's consciousness of these *a priori* principles, unless he too appeals to a sanction, in which case he too becomes utilitarian.[3] This applies even if the sanction be no more than the unhappiness of not having followed one's conscience. For, thus regarded, conscience is

---

[1] James F. Stephen, *Liberty, Equality, Fraternity*, 1873. Cambridge University Press (ed. White), 1967.

[2] *Op. cit.* p.283.

[3] *Ibid.* p.280.

> a motive... and if it is regarded as a motive, it must come into competition with other motives, and so the utilitarian answer to the question, "Why should I do right?" must be given.

Apart from this sanction the "sense of duty... would be simply an irrational, instinctive shrinking from a particular set of acts" which one might do well to overcome.[4] That is, one might have a duty to overcome a sense of duty so conceived, as Huck Finn had a duty, in following his natural niceness, to overcome his inbred if not innate sense that he should not help the runaway slave-boy.

Stephen goes on, however, to make a distinction. He singles out a second kind of belief in moral intuitions claimed, as opposed to the principle of expediency, to be the ultimate justification of moral principles. This belief is more than "not an answer at all", as was the sense of duty ploy. It involves commitments "which utilitarians are interested in denying."

> Unless those who believe in moral intuitions go so far as to assert the existence of specific moral rules expressed in a definite form of distinctly intelligible words, capable of being applied at once to human conduct, and perceived by some specific faculty of the mind to be absolute unvarying ultimate truths, they assert nothing which utilitarians are interested in denying.

Here Stephen does two things at once. He tells us that what utilitarians would deny is that there are "specific moral rules" and he also enumerates the difficulties with such an account, adding for good measure that "Probably no one in these days would make such an assertion," though he does not indicate who in other days might have done so.

Stephen would deny that his principle of utility obliges in the same way as he thinks that the believer in the "existence of specific moral rules" envisages such rules as obliging him, as his discussion of "ought"[5] makes clear. For the latter (we might call him the intuitionist) speaks of rules in that he imagines them to oblige independently of any end to be gained by their observance, an attitude which we may remember from our childhood. It is difficult to see, though, why this would not be true of the *principle* of utility, i.e. that it would oblige as a rule not serving any further end, if there is not to be an endless regress and if metaphysics are to be eschewed. In fact the utilitarian principle serves and is directed to the extrinsic principle of happiness, i.e. of aggregate happiness, neither exclusively one's own nor yet a truly common good. But no reason is given why we *should* serve this end. It seems just to be enjoined in the familiar intuitionist way. Hence the protests of ethical "egoism".

---

[4] It is interesting to note here that the same objection can be made to *a priori* principles in the theoretical sphere. There is no reason to think them true unless we see the truth of them now, in which case they are not *a priori*. On the sense of duty in this negative sense, cf. P.T. Geach, "The Moral Law and the Law of God" in *God and the Soul*, London 1969.

[5] *Ibid.* pp.277-279.

The difficulties Stephen raises against the absolutist intuitionism which he opposes, as if it were the *sole* alternative to utilitarianism, are, first, the general difficulty of relating thoughts to language, second, that of recognizing instances where a principle applies, third, the problem of knowing whether one truly perceives the principles as existing.

Stephen might seem to have in mind, as alternative to utilitarianism in this second sense, an acceptance of the Ten Commandments or even of the two commandments of the Gospel, viz. love of God and neighbour. But this would mean that many, even a majority of people, in his day as in ours, "make such an assertion", contrary to his claim that probably no one would do so. Moreover, such commandments do not need to be "perceived by some specific faculty of the mind to be absolute", since as commandments they are merely received as from a divine authority. So it is more likely that his target is or ought to be some form of philosophical Kantianism, at least assimilable, however, as he sees it, to unreflective religious attitudes.

He wishes perhaps to isolate the common factor uniting these approaches to morals in opposition to utilitarianism. For there is, in the same way, one negative element common in turn to all forms of utilitarianism, viz. the denial that there is any law, in the world or in conscience, to which men must bow just because it is promulgated by an authority to which respect is due. Utilitarianism is as such offered as commending itself to men of good sense on purely speculative grounds. One speculates *about* the practical matter of finding a rule of behaviour. The Judaeo-Christian ethic, on the other hand, is essentially a matter of commands and of the obligation to obey them. Even the spiritual law of love is promulgated as a command.[6]

It is thus not to the point for Mill to have written that "In the golden rule of Jesus of Nazareth we read the complete spirit of the ethics of utility,"[7] even if that had been true. For "everybody to count for one, nobody for more than one" was precisely the utilitarian arithmetic upon which Caiaphas defended the expediency of encompassing the death of Christ, an expediency which, in company with Mill and Bentham, he appears in general to have identified with the morally right. As we know, the Evangelist took this pronouncement as being prophetically true, but in the different sense that it was expedient for Christ to sacrifice himself, which was permissible and indeed supremely praiseworthy, whereas his murder on utilitarian grounds remained impermissible[8], and this illustrates our

---

[6] This remains so even if the Christian claim be of a revelation that the point, the *end* of all commands, all precepts, is the glory of God and the redemption of man, necessarily in that order. On a theistic scheme divine sovereignty, and hence commands, have to be involved.

[7] Quoted in Stephen, *op. cit.* p.222.

[8] The true moral arithmetic, rather, as Kant appears to have appreciated, is that everyone should count for all and none for less than all. This enshrines the truth that the *common* good is harmed by murder.

claim that the divine law is grounded upon, since it indeed includes, the highest expediency, of which however we ourselves have no right to an initially perfect understanding.

So the point we are making here is that the utilitarian ethic, unlike the ethics of Jesus, is radically anti-religious, since it rejects any form of authoritative curb or, better, guidance upon the exercise, in individual living men, of practical reason. A man should do what seems to him expedient, whether for himself or for society, it tells us; that *is* the morally right.

Now this is even in a sense, by our own position, true. But it is understood as basic to utilitarianism that what is expedient is not to be interpreted in terms of, for example, what is just, so that *any* act of injustice will irreparably harm the perpetrator's participation in the common good (as it also harms the common good itself). The norms of justice, rather, are only to be followed in so far as they can be seen to be expedient. It would seem, all the same, that the notion of utilitarianism could be widened to embrace a teleological metaphysics of morals which could serve as a foundation for absolute moral precepts. It is expedient, it might then be claimed, to recognize absolute precepts, and even truth itself need not, indeed cannot, be divorced from the beneficial, just as it is the *veracity* of the senses which aid the animal's survival.[9] The original "practical" utilitarianism could then be rejected as a distorted reaction against the false, Kantian metaphysics of morals. For according to this wider programme the notions of the *bonum honestum* and of the spiritually beautiful, most literally applicable only to God himself, take their place within a general teleological scheme.

It is not merely the promulgated laws of revelation, however, which what we might call Victorian utilitarianism rejects, while maybe appearing to coincide with them at certain points. It rejects, is "interested in denying", says Stephen, the rights and duties of conscience, the "specific moral rules" which people acknowledge as binding, except where such bonds are judged expedient for getting what is wanted.

One might imagine accepting the commandments of scripture in religious obedience, while at the same time adopting the criterion of utility for all conscientious dealings not touched on by those commandments. This would be a ham-handed groping after the doctrine of prudence (*phronesis*) outlined in Aristotle and elaborated on in the moral theology of Aquinas but by those who had lost all *rapport* with the riches of the tradition. One difficulty straight off is that the divine commandments themselves are understood, in their own tra-

[9] See our "Meaning in a Realist Perspective", *The Thomist* 55, January 1991, pp.29-51, esp.pp.50-51.

dition, as leaving no area of life untouched. They are intended as a complete guide. This do, i.e. live thus, and thou shalt live, as scripture reports the voice of God or of his messenger Moses. This statement does not of itself suggest that the access of life is what makes the doing of them right. The commandments themselves, rather, we have argued, must be understood as internally directed to goods, of which life is one. Hence the doing of the commandments *in order to have life* is more encouraged than otherwise, and this motivation is not of course excluded from the later "He who seeks to save his life will lose it", as can be shown from context. Still, the giving of life is not what is *meant* by the commandments being right, even if it is always right to do what brings life.[10] This is the point of Maritain's distinctions between formal and final causality in morals, between the order of specification and the order of exercise.

Maritain[11] compares the honourable good (*bonum honestum*) in the moral order to substance in the metaphysical order. As substance is "the first meaning of being in the order of the categories", so the honourable good is "what is desirable or loveable in itself" in the moral order, i.e. it is the fullness of being of "the act of freedom itself" as agreeing with its own rule, viz. reason. It is necessary however to see that the moral "order" is in reality situated within the one and only real order, ultimately the "metaphysical" order. Then we can see that virtue is only *called* the honourable good or that which is to be enjoyed (*frui*, not merely *utile*) in itself as being that which is more known to us than is the supreme and only really honourable good, viz. God, beatitude, happiness (*felicitas*),[12] to which virtue leads and in which it in some way can participate.

There are in fact theologians who maintain that the only law is the law of love, which, like the utilitarian principle, may prescribe action now in one way now in another, without regard for any principle other than itself. The chief objection to this view though is that if there are no principles of what is of value, even of inviolable value, other than love itself then there can be no basis upon which love can go to work. It can have no worthy object. Even if human beings be declared to be ends in some unexplained sense, yet there would be no way of loving them if nothing *else* were of value, i.e. of moral value as bearing upon their free activity, for these human beings, e.g. if they did not acknowledge an imperative to preserve innocent life, their own or another's.

---

[10] Cf. our *Morals as Founded on Natural Law*, Peter Lang, Frankfurt 1987, ch.2.

[11] *Op. cit.* p.40.

[12] In the discussion of the *bonum honestum, Summa theol.* IIa-IIae QQ143-145, Aquinas seems to use these three terms interchangeably. It is noteworthy that he makes *honestas* (with *verecundia*) an integral part specifically of temperance, equating it with what he calls spiritual beauty, recalling Maritain's reference to *formal* causality in this connection, since beauty is of the form. Temperance, of course, and chastity in particular, is a virtue which the utilitarian approach makes particularly difficult to appreciate (though it does not entirely overthrow it, as it does justice).

The relevance, anyhow, of this consideration is that the objection can be brought in parallel against utilitarianism. How can anything be useful if nothing is given value and unconditional respect? How can even happiness receive any consistently defensible content? Aquinas, by contrast, finds no difficulty in declaring love to be the form of all virtue and yet assigning to various forms of behaviour each their specific good and object. Love, indeed, as seeking the good of another seeks its perfection, and perfection is necessarily perfection of a nature, of what that thing is. So love is not separable from nature, here human nature, as, in its perfectibility, being the end of all virtue as of all love itself.

The utilitarians, we found, were still caught up in the Kantian world against which they were reacting. Here moral principles are as it were *sui generis* in relation to the larger class of practical principles directed towards practical ends. Thomists, of course, distinguish practical activity concerned with *factibilia* (the province of *ars* or *techne*) from that concerned with *agibilia* (the province of the moral virtues). In Kantianism, however, the moral principles are furnished with no end whatever. Moral good no longer has a foundation in extra-mental reality; it is a purely formal quality of reason which, if anything, would *make* its object good, impossible though this be. So much is this so that even commands enunciated by a divine authority would *ipso facto* lack the inward purity of moral principle, since such authority would be, it is assumed, heteronomous. Hence successors of Kant such as G.E. Moore think to refute divine authority, and by implication the *lex aeterna*, by pointing to the *formal* (in a logical sense) possibility of asking whether God is good. This merely illustrates the total separation from metaphysics in which such ethicists work. The separation is taken as a praiseworthy professional principle but it is in fact a wilful blindness, stemming from a phenomenalist failure to appreciate the difference between what is distinguishable and what is necessarily separate. One cannot fail, in addition, to detect the baneful influence of the fourteenth century voluntarist theologians behind this whole approach. God, by his absolute power, can create separately whatever can be conceived separately, we remember Ockham as saying, possibly deriving encouragement from Scotus's doctrine of the *distinctio formalis a parte rei*, again a claim to a distinction in the thing wherever there is a distinction in the mind. Although this was, for Scotus, an attempt to defend the reality, the realism, of knowledge, its effect was to initiate an unravelling of the whole Aristotelian insistence upon the difference between the way things are found in the mind and the way they are found in reality, this in turn having been the only way in which true science of the perpetual flux of changing things could have been established as a possibility after the criticisms of material reality offered by the Ionians and even by Plato. It was mere deference to this development when the arch-sceptic Hume applied the same principle, viz. "Whatever is conceivable is possible", with a parallel destructiveness. But he in turn got it from that old Ockhamist, Descartes, the "father of modern philosophy".

When this Ockhamist scepticism was applied to ethics, as by Kant (a taking of what is conceivable in separation from metaphysics as always really possible, so that no law can be laid down, but only a series of "as ifs"), then it cried out to be discredited. This climate is what enabled the Victorian judge, Stephen, to say that probably no one "would assert the existence of moral rules" any more, in apparent disregard of the principles of Christian life of which he elsewhere shows himself so aware. He is thinking, doubtless, of moral imperatives divorced from all justifying purpose, somehow reigning in men's consciousness and demanding subjection to them.

Kantianism and utilitarianism, then, are alike absurd, due to the lack of any theory of value, of ends determining and indeed specifying the prescribed actions as being their object(s). This situation is not remedied by a hasty substitution of pleasure for the happiness variable, since this is like stipulating that the value of x be y, i.e. an equally unknown quantity, one indeed requiring a long analysis which if diligently and exactly pursued would lead the utilitarian back into those Aristotelian and Thomistic postures from which he imagines himself to have taken flight.

There is a third possibility not considered by Stephen. There may exist in reality certain permanent proportions knowable by the intellect, which would express them in conceptual and verbal formulae, such as moral rules or precepts. This proportion would not be divorced from purpose or even from "matters of fact", for this proportion, which would be common to all such relations captured by enunciated precepts, would be the *iustum*, or just thing, as bearing upon that which is *iustum*, just. It would be, like everything else, discoverable empirically, but as an *a posteriori* necessity, such as, on the same account, would be the laws of logic and first principles in general.[13] The proportion would be one of identity between a given action or, eventually, type of action and the quality of being *faciendum*, i.e. to be done, or, of course, *evitandum*, to be avoided.[14] The unspoken purpose, of course, is the perfection of

[13] Cf. Aristotle, *Post. An.* II 17.

[14] This anyhow would be the so to say final proportion, corresponding to the first, ever-guiding precept of natural law, *bonum est persequendum*. Prior to that is the proportion between any being and its perception as an end, that is to say, as a good, of which a sub-class would be that of actions performable by a free agent and the perception of their eventual performance as a desirable end, i.e. as a good. These actions are what are morally good and so the habits enabling us to perform them are moral habits or virtues. There is a certain secondariness of level here, however, since actions themselves considered as realities or (accidental) beings, prior to the goodness or badness of their performance, consist in a relation between the relevant change (*motus*) in the agent and the good sought, which as object indeed specifies the action. What then distinguishes an action from a simple truth that a given thing, say money or food, is good is the factor of pursuit, of the act of will, internal and external, entailing change in the agent. We distinguish here, therefore, the statement that debts are to be paid from the secondary judgment that

the agent. It is only a being in a situation of imperfection, of potentiality, of not being perfected, which can and has to be an agent (unless, as in the case of an infinite being, its agency or act is one with its primal act of being itself).

These relations, anyhow, these proportions, may exist and constitute a charter of duties for the agent concerned as part of his programme of living out his life, of becoming what he is set by nature to be. This brings us back to our central topic of natural law, one frowned upon, it would seem, by Mr. Justice Stephen, who is nonetheless, like Thomas Hobbes before him, a valuable ally in many respects.

Natural law is a historically identifiable body of theory, which has received its classical shape at the hands of certain individuals. It would therefore be rather disingenuous to pretend to discover it for the first time, and so there is nothing "derivative" in any derogatory sense in following the tradition here.

The discussion in Stephen's book, indeed, appears somewhat flawed. On the one hand one finds talk of precepts not imposed for any end, while on the other one finds denial of there being any precepts at all, this denial being seen as a consequence of admitting the importance of ends. But if it indeed belongs to the concept of an obligation that it is imposed for some end then the absurdity of both these positions becomes apparent, as indeed does the contemporary dilemma presented in some quarters between teleological and deontological ethics.

*

*   *

Utilitarianism, we found, appears to be an extreme reaction against Kantian and other forms of intuitionism. It is arguable that it departs at least as far from the norm as they do, and in view of its secularist history and character it seems misplaced to suggest that "the utilitarian is the natural ally of the Christian." If, moreover, the custom had never grown up of understanding the absoluteness of obligation as meaning that it obliges without teleological reference (instead of meaning that there is, absolutely, in the type of situation concerned, no other way of coming at the end), then utility would never have been proposed as the antithesis of obligation. As Aquinas observed, the *bonum utile* and the *bonum honestum* more often than not coincide *in re* (as in the end they do completely), though they differ *in ratione*. What is wrong or unjust cannot be useful, while what is truly beneficial, *sub specie aeternitatis* at least, cannot be wrong or unjust.

---

the paying of debts is good (as an action), in order to point out that the meaning of *bonum* in *bonum est persequendum* encompasses not only good actions but that just proportion, as between a debt and its payment, a child and its education, a neighbour and one's love, realised *in* and as the aim of a good action. Beyond that, even, the good as such (*bonum in communi*, one with the Last End) is pursued as natural object of the will.

Now it does not follow that to understand an obligation one has to understand what its end is. That would undercut the parental power to lay obligations upon their uncomprehending but, let us hope, properly obedient children. What we assert is, more simply, that understanding what an obligation is involves understanding that it is imposed for some end. Parents who pretended to impose motiveless obligations upon their children could only be supposed to have wicked motives, such as cruel deception, since the child presumes, in the nature of things, that there is some good parental reason for the unpleasant things he is made to do. He believes, in other words, in the *wisdom* of his parents. One does not wish by this, however, to exclude the possibility that the child starts off with only a partial understanding of what obligation is, similar indeed to what in the adult intuitionist we reckon to be a misunderstanding. Hence what is pejoratively irrational in maturity may be a survival of what was once legitimately sub-rational. In this case, anyhow, one would want to say that the child's coming more and more to see the point of his duties for himself gives him motivation for an ever more assiduous obedience, whatever contradictions may appear in the dialectical psychology of growing up.

The voluntarist defender of absolute obligation may appeal to the scriptural passages we cited in support of our own position against the utilitarians, as if they spoke for him. But in fact they paramountly exemplify our conclusion already reached that absoluteness of precept must rest upon the absolute desirability of some end. Thus in the Biblical scheme of things the supreme end is God, the aim of life to be right with Him. But this is not necessarily to say that every precept is imposed solely with a view to God. The Israelites were told to be faithful in marriage because the good of just marriage on its own cannot be preserved without such a habit and this is what makes it right and *a fortiori* good. To switch the reasoning to the foundations of the goodness of marriage itself would be to take up another topic.

A difference from the secular theories emerges here. There the explanation of experience is almost always distorted by an urge to reduce the explanation to the scope of one idea, as a "working model" again, be it expediency, pleasure or the categorical imperative. That is why these systems are more truly regarded as ideologies of morals than as metaphysical analyses of them. There is a disregard for reality, a defective interest in it, under pressure, perhaps, of the urge to dominate and control.

The theistic scheme of things, on the other hand, implies no such idolatry of ideas as against reality. For it is just God, supreme end and first cause, who *gives* value to the other things, marriage, pleasure, good moral action, a household pet, victory in a just cause, which can occur as ends conferring obligatoriness upon human actions. So whereas the supreme end, creator of the world, diffuses his value over the world, good as the cause of good, cause as the source of a real secondary causality, the chief end of the secularist, pleasure, purity of race, production, duty, on the other hand, is typically adopted in a fanatical manner, as sucking all value up into itself and leaving the world empty. Thus, paradoxically, even Hare's scheme of things, conceived as a protection against fanatics (against whom, paradoxically again, he professes to have no *argument*, urging that they will "always be few"), has a distinctly fanatical constrictiveness about it as he triumphantly asks us where we are going to flee from his indeed "meagre" concepts.

To defend the theistic view philosophically (i.e. non-voluntaristically[15]) one has to introduce what was called, e.g. by Augustine, the Eternal Law, i.e. the *ratio divinae sapientiae*, essence (or, so to say, coefficient) of the divine wisdom, "directing the motions and acts of everything." This necessity indeed would follow immediately upon the explanatory definition of natural law by Aquinas as simply "the sharing of the Eternal Law by intelligent creatures." This indeed is its justification as law. If there were no Eternal Law there would be no basis for the divine commands or for ethical obligations, though it might still be prudential to follow them.[16]

The notion of God itself dissolves if we try to conceive of an arbitary will, instead of a God acting in accordance with the eternal understanding of Himself. If will is definitionally an inclination to the understood good (even in human beings it is an inclination of the substantive intellect itself) then an arbitrary will is equivalent to an absence of will. Just as God is His wisdom, so the *lex aeterna* must also be God as ordering all things, including the precepts of human practical reason or natural law. It orders the latter in a special or privileged way, however, in so far as natural law, reason, is "a reflected divine light", man as spiritual being made to the divine image, able to investigate the being of all things in their own reality. The intellect, says Aristotle, "comes from outside".

The doctrine means that the question whether God has perhaps decreed some evil to be good, as imagined by Moore, *cannot* be raised, however grammatical it might seem (one can after all suggest, grammatically, that ice is not frozen water or that John is smoking Mary). On the other hand God as God could not be bound to standards outside Himself. The voluntarists, concerned to deny this, tried to reconstruct God in the image of a *creature* bound by no standards, but with unlimited power. The truth is that God *is* His standard. He

---

[15] I am not suggesting that theology is, in contrast, necessarily voluntaristic. Good theology can only be in harmony with the findings of philosophy (though it in turn can guide philosophy to its own fruition, as history shows).

[16] On the theistic view indeed it is also supremely prudential to follow the divine commands, so as not to be exposed to eternal failure and self-destruction, but beyond that, beyond human redemption, as already remarked, lies the final motivation of the divine glorification ("hallowed be thy name"), a religious concept, if anything is, without which, however, obligation formally freed of anything "hypothetical" cannot be finally explained. Even this concept, however, as related to the necessary sovereignty of an infinite being, can be philosophically defended.

would have to be. This does not mean that God is literally obliged by Himself, since obligation can apply only to finite creatures. God is not obliged to keep promises; it belongs to the *ratio* of God that He does keep them.

It might seem that on our view theodicy is essential to moral theory, at least of that "modern" sort which G.E.M. Anscombe's 1958 article (in *Philosophy*) discussed. Stephen, for example, argues that belief in God without conviction as to a future state would not make a comparable difference to people's assent to moral principles, and one can understand by "assent" here an assent to their truth. They would not be *justified* as rational, for the way we should behave if we have an eternal destiny is indeed different from how we should behave if we did not, just as true sexual morality would be entirely different if sex were not of itself (i.e. by nature) connected with reproduction. This would mean that the moral philosopher who would defend the values reckoned traditional (as distinct from some variant on the Nietzschean programme, say) would also be committed to arguing for "a future state". Stephen, however, might be wrong on the point of fact. The Jews under the Old Covenant had no such explicit belief in a future state.

What *is* necessary, and it follows from belief in an omnipotent, just and merciful God, is the conviction that justice and mercy will prevail *in some way or other* (we may think of Mother Julian's proclaimed belief that "all shall be well", conjoined beyond her understanding with her acceptance on other grounds of the doctrine of eternal punishment). One need not deny, however, that one might fail to see this and yet continue to practise virtue out of love for its intrinsic value, apprehended before or without that its necessary foundation in the *lex aeterna* is grasped. But the question remains as to whether a powerless God would be ultimately authoritative. The taste for virtue might then be nothing more than a taste, and possibly a perverted taste in so far as one would lack hope of attaining the good ends which give virtue their shape; these ends, after all, the Marxists were surely right in arguing, are common to society or to the human race, and cannot be made dependent upon individual luck. This noble view, however, conflicts with what they must view as the irremediable bad luck suffered by many, at least, of the dead, i.e. if one disdains their ideological view that an individual is worthless.

Hope, then, is internal to virtue. Not to hope, then, seems to be to fail in virtue, as indeed the moralists have taught. But what minimum is needed to give a sure or at least a possible foundation to the kind of hope required is an important question for humanity. Nor should one exclude in advance that what philosophy or other investigations might uncover could be more than such a bare minimum.

Index

Bibliography

Classical or standard works are not listed.

ANSCOMBE, G.E.M., "A Reply to Mr. C.S. Lewis's Argument that 'Naturalism' is Self-Refuting", *Socratic Digest* No. 4, 1948.

—, "Modern Moral Philosophy", *Philosophy*: London 1958.

BOURKE, V., "The Synderesis Rule and Right Reason", *The Monist* 66, No. 1, January 1983.

DAWSON, C., *Religion and Culture*, Sheed & Ward: London 1948.

DENNETT, D., *Brainstorms*, Bradford Books: Montgomery 1978.

DONAGAN, A., *The Theory of Morality*, University of Chicago Press: Chicago & London 1977.

ELDERS, L., "St. Thomas Aquinas' Doctrine of Conscience", *Lex et Libertas*, Libreria Editrice Vaticana: Vatican City 1987.

—, *The Metaphysics of Being of St. Thomas Aquinas*, Brill: Leyden 1993.

FINNIS, J., *Natural Law and Natural Rights*, Clarendon Press: Oxford 1980.

FOOT, P., "Morality and Art", Henrietta Hertz Lecture, *Proceedings of the British Academy* LVI, London 1970.

—, "When is a Principle a Moral Principle?" *Aristotelian Society Supplement* XXVIII: London 1954.

FUCHS, J., *Natural Law*, Gill: Dublin 1965.

GEACH, P.T., *God and the Soul*, RKP: London 1969.

—, "Teleological Explanation", *Explanation* (ed. S. Körner), Blackwell: Oxford 1976.

—, *The Virtues*, Cambridge University Press: Cambridge 1976.

— (with ANSCOMBE, G.E.M.), *Three Philosophers*, Blackwells: Oxford 1967.

GILSON, E., *The Spirit of Medieval Philosophy*, Scribners: New York 1940.

GRABMANN, M., *Thomas von Aquin*, Munich 1959.

GRISEZ, G., "The First Principle of Practical Reason" (abridged version), *Aquinas: a Collection of Critical Essays* (ed. A. Kenny), Macmillan, London 1969.

HARE, R.M., *Freedom and Reason*, Clarendon Press: Oxford 1963.

—, *The Language of Morals*, Oxford University Press: Oxford 1952.

HILDEBRAND, D: von, *Christian Ethics*, Thames & Hudson: London 1953.

HUNTFORD, R., *The New Totalitarians*, Penguin: London 1971.

KEKES, J., "Happiness", *Mind*, July 1982.

LEWIS, C.S., *Miracles*, Bles: London 1947.

—, *The Abolition of Man*, Bles: London 1943.

MACINTYRE, A.C., *After Virtue*, Duckworth: London 1981.

MARITAIN, J., An Introduction to Philosophy*, Sheed & Ward: London 1933.*

—, *Christianity and Democracy*, Bles: London 1945.

—, *Neuf Lecons sur les notions premières de la philosophie morale*, Pierre Tequi: Paris 1950 (transl. *An Introduction to the Basic Problems of Moral Philosophy*, Magi Books: Albany 1990).

MCCABE, H., *Law, Love and Language* (in the U.S.A., *What is Ethics all About?), Sheed & Ward (Facet Books): London 1968.*

MCDOWELL, J., "Virtue and Reason", *The Monist* 1979.

MCINERNY, R:, *Ethica Thomistica, Catholic University of America Press: Washington 1982.*

MEYNELL, H., "Doubts about Wittgenstein's Influence", *Philosophy*: London 1981.
MONTMARQUET, J., "Nagel on Motivation", *Australasian Journal of Philosophy*, March 1982.
MURALT, A. de, "The Founded Act and the Apperception of Others", *The Self and Others* (ed. Tymeniecka), Dordrecht 1977.
NAGEL, T., *The Possibility of Altruism*, Oxford 1970.
NOWELL-SMITH, P.H., *Ethics*, Pelican: London 1954.
SARTRE, J.-P., *Being and Nothingness* (tr. H. Barnes), Washington Square Press, New York 1966 (*L'être et le néant*, Gallimard: Paris 1943).
SCHÖRNBORN, C., "L'homme créé par Dieu: le fondement de la dignité de l'homme", *Gregorianum*: Rome 1984.
SEANOR, D. (and FOTION, N.), *Hare and Critics: Essays on Moral Thinking*, Clarendon Press: Oxford 1988.
SIDGWICK, H., *The Methods of Ethics* (1874), Dover: New York 1966.
SMITH, J., "Can Virtue Be in the Service of Bad Acts: a Response to Philippa Foot", *The New Scholasticism* 1984.
SNARE, F., "Dissolving the Moral Contract", *Philosophy*: London, July 1977.
SPAEMANN, R., "Über den Begriff der Menschenwürde", *Scheidewege* 15, 1985/6.
STEPHEN, J.F., *Liberty, Equality, Fraternity* (1873), Cambridge University Press: Cambridge 1967.
STEVENSON, C., *Ethics and Language*, Yale University Press: Newhaven 1944.
THERON, S., *Africa, Philosophy and the Western Tradition*, Peter Lang: Frankfurt 1995.
—, "Meaning in a Realist Perspective", *The Thomist* 55, January 1991.
—, *Morals as Founded on Natural Law*, Peter Lang: Frankfurt 1987.
—, *Philosophy or Dialectic?* Peter Lang: Frankfurt 1994.
—, "St. Thomas Aquinas and epieicheia", *Lex et Libertas* (ed. Elders & Hedwig), Libreria Editrice Vaticana: Vatican City 1987.
—, "The Moral Law and Theism", *The Thomist*, January 1983.
—, *The Recovery of Purpose*, Peter Lang: Frankfurt 1993.
TOCQUEVILLE, A. de, *Democracy in America* (1830), Mentor: New York 1956.
URMSON, J.O., "On Grading", *Mind* 1950.
VEATCH, H., "Are there Non-Moral Goods?" *The New Scholasticism*, Autumn 1978.
—, *Human Rights: Fact or Fancy?* Louisiana State University Press: Baton Rouge & London 1985.
—, *Rational Man*, Bloomington 1962.
WALGRAVE, J., "Reason and Will in Natural Law", *Lex et Libertas* (ed. Elders & Hedwig), Libreria Editrice Vaticana: Vatican City 1987.

PRINTED ON PERMANENT PAPER • IMPRIME SUR PAPIER PERMANENT • GEDRUKT OP DUURZAAM PAPIER - ISO 9706
ORIENTALISTE, KLEIN DALENSTRAAT 42, B-3020 HERENT